All images are copyrighted © and rights are reserved by their creators.
Images not donated by restaurants featured are copyright © noted through
gettyimages.com, pixabay.com, unsplash.com, or wikipedia.org (unless otherwise indicated).
Back Cover: Catfish, Berry's Seafood and Catfish House

Mississippi
BACK ROAD RESTAURANT
Recipes

A Cookbook & Restaurant Guide

ANITA MUSGROVE

Great American Cookbooks
www.GreatAmericanPublishers.com
TOLL-FREE 1-888-854-5954

Recipe Collection © 2021 by Great American Publishers
ALL RIGHTS RESERVED
All rights reserved, including the right of reproduction in whole or in part in any form.

ISBN 978-1-934817-52-0

by Anita Musgrove

Layout and design by Maria Shedd

First Edition

10 9 8 7 6 5 4 3 2 1

Proud member of:
GENUINE MS

Great American Cookbooks
171 Lone Pine Church Road • Lena, MS 39094
TOLL-FREE 1.888.854.5954 • www.GreatAmericanPublishers.com

Every effort has been made to ensure the accuracy of the information provided in this book. However, dates, times, and locations are subject to change. Please call locations or visit websites for up-to-date information before traveling.

To purchase books in quantity for corporate use, incentives, or fundraising, please call Great American Cookbooks at 888-854-5954.

CONTENTS

PREFACE	6
DELTA REGION	10
HILLS REGION	42
PINES CHAPTER	82
CAPITAL REGION	122
COASTAL REGION	190
RESTAURANT INDEX	240
RECIPE INDEX	246

home sweet home

Author Anita (left) with her sister Nedra.

PREFACE

HELLO TRAVEL BUDDIES Our latest adventure takes us throughout the Magnolia State eating at the best restaurants known to man… locally owned restaurants of Mississippi. This is the tenth book in my BACK ROAD RESTAURANT RECIPES SERIES. We have traveled through Alabama, Kentucky, Tennessee, Texas, Missouri, Louisiana, South Carolina, North Carolina, Oklahoma, and now my home state of Mississippi. Although I was born in Alabama, I like to call Mississippi home because this is where I have spent most of my life.

In 1959, my father, Ray Cantrell Sr. was awarded a contract to open a shirt business in Brandon. For almost a year, I had the pleasure of making trips with him to bring supplies and payroll to the new employees. We finally found a house on Pleasant Street in Brandon in March 1960. That Easter weekend, I had a choice of staying home to help pack or traveling to Brandon with Daddy. I chose Daddy, of course. I was always Daddy's girl. The only furniture in our new house was a bedside table and a bed, but on the floor by the bed was the biggest Easter basket I had ever seen. And the eggs were all hidden just for me. An Easter egg hunt all to myself, my Daddy all to myself, and Easter Service in a church that made my little country church in Alabama look like a dollhouse… what more could a 10-year-old want?

In those days, Brandon was just a small town east of Jackson. It was the kind of town where you knew everyone and everyone knew you, where Momma and Daddy would know about any trouble before you ever made it home for supper. Speaking of supper, in my house you better be sitting at the table and ready to eat by the time Momma had it on the table, and dishes were done as soon as we finished eating. My older sister Nedra would wash the dishes and I would dry because drying meant you were the last to leave the kitchen and had to sweep the floors before the lights were turned off. I remember taking off on my bike in the early mornings and playing football in our big yard with all the neighborhood kids. I even had my first crush on the boy that always seemed to be the only one who could tackle me, and had my first real kiss at the end of one of those tackles.

If you have read any of my previous books you know I am a sunrise and sunset girl. I also love to be outdoors savoring the aroma of burning leaves in the fall and driving down Mississippi country roads watching leaves blowing behind the car in front of me as if they are dancing to a tune all of their own. The golds and reds are always so beautiful as I look across the open fields to the tree line. My daughter, Sheila, has obviously inherited this love of the back roads. She will occasionally call me up for a quick day trip after hearing me mention a place I haven't seen in a while or a desire to visit my parents, old homeplace or to eat at a restaurant from my past. These are memories that last forever.

That is one thing I love about locally owned restaurants. It may have been ten years since you last visited but turn the corner and there they are. There may be a little more rust on the sign and the benches out front may be a little more worn, but open the doors and the aromas from the kitchen hit you like they did the first time you went to eat. Familiar places, familiar faces, and the foods you loved growing up is what makes locally owned restaurants so much a part of our communities and our life.

Mississippi is blessed with the best of the best locally owned places to eat. For our tour, we'll start at the top in the Delta Region where I love to fish and visit old friends with my traveling buddy, Richard Shaw. Richard has lived and farmed all over the Delta Region and our visits there have renewed my love of fishing. We especially enjoy Lake Washington and the thrill of pulling out the big crappies. Most people traveling the Delta Region have two things on their mind—blues and good food. The Delta is the land where the blues began, Rock and Roll was created, and Gospel remains a vibrant art. It is home to music greats like B.B. King, Muddy Waters, "Son" House Jr., and Robert Johnson to name a few. Actor James Earl Jones was also from the Delta. While in the area, be sure to eat at **The Crystal Grill**, a Greenwood gem for Southern food done right. **Scott's Hot Tamales** in Greenville is the place for tamales that have been made from the same recipe since 1950.

Author Anita's Grandbabies, Brooke, Morgan, and Bryce.

The Hills Region, rich in agriculture and talent, was home to Elvis Presley. Once known as "the Hillbilly Cat," Elvis sang blues, country, pop, and gospel. He broke all the girls' hearts when he stood up for his country and joined the Army and had his hair cut. You can visit the Elvis Presley Birthplace and Museum in Tupelo. Oxford is the home of American novelist William Faulkner where you can tour his home, Rowan Oak. While in Oxford, eat at **Ajax Diner** for award-winning good eats from steak to meatloaf to Southern fried chicken. In Como at **Como Steakhouse**, the juicy steaks are aged 27 days, cut by hand, and grilled to perfection atop a charcoal-fired, open-pit grill.

Dropping down to the Pines Region, we will travel through French Camp and visit **Council House Restaurant.** The Council House was originally the meeting place for Greenwood LeFlore—the last chief of the Choctaw Indian Nation east of the Mississippi—and his chiefs during tribal negotiations. Visit for good food, outside dining on the deck in front of a fireplace, and their famous French Camp bread. In Meridian, plan a stop at the Jimmie Rodgers Museum. An intimate museum with historical artifacts and instruments from legendary musician, Jimmie Rodgers, known as the Father of Country Music. Another great stop is the Highland Park Dentzel Carousel and Shelter Building, The carousel was manufactured about 1896 for the 1904 St. Louis Exposition by the Dentzel Carousel Company of Philadelphia, Pennsylvania, and was sold and shipped to Meridian after the fair. If you're in search of old-fashioned comfort food, **The Checker Board** is the place to be. Located just off the interstate, they are open seven days a week for buffet-style lunch and breakfast. You're sure to leave satisfied but dreaming about your next trip back; I know because this is one of mine and Sheila's favorite places to stop when we get an early start and are looking for a great breakfast.

Author Anita and daughter, Sheila Simmons.

The Capital Region is where I live, and believe me, I haunt the locally owned places to eat. They know me by name and can usually order my food before I get inside. **Boo's Smokehouse Bar-B-Que**, central Mississippi's premier barbecue restaurant, is one of those places. I went to school with Boo, and when he found out I was writing *Mississippi Back Road Restaurant Recipes*, he said he wanted to be the first in the book. Boo's Smokehouse Bar-B-Que is so good, you'll "hug the cook and kiss the pig." Further south, close to Mendenhall and near the Strong River, **Eason's Fish House** serves the best catfish, turnip greens, and homemade hushpuppies you ever tasted. The food is always hot, and they have the best service around. Candy keeps an eye on perfection in the food and the service.

The casinos and beaches of the Coastal region bring travelers from across the world. When my grandson, Bryce, learned I started the Mississippi book, he was excited to tell me about **Letha's Bar-B-Que Inn** in Petal. He said they have to be in the book because they serve the best barbecue he has ever tasted. Ms. Letha began serving her barbecue in the 1970s, and her family continues her legacy by serving tender ribs that fall off the bone, slow-cooked pulled pork, smoked sausage, smoked chicken, and homemade sides. **Murky Waters** is a fun hangout for locals and newcomers. All three locations—Hattiesburg, Gulfport, and Ocean Springs—feature award-winning barbecue, local craft brews, and authentic live blues music. Be sure to save time to visit the Institute for Marine Mammal Studies, a nonprofit organization established in 1984 for the purposes of public education, conservation, and research on marine mammals and sea turtles in the wild and under human care. It is a fun and educational experience of a lifetime—an absolute must-do if you are in the area.

I thank God for giving me this opportunity to bring another book into print and to share it with so many readers. My team deserves all the credit due them for the many hours of hard work it takes to bring a book like this to life. Maria Shedd and Tasha Monk are the best production team ever. Our sales team, Amber Feiock, Rachael Dean, and Casey Weeks, work hard to get our books from the warehouse into the hands of readers. Office manager, Diane Rothery, keeps our GAP world turning; we would be lost without her. Our leaders, Roger and Sheila Simmons keep us on track with a tender and gentle hand. It is rare in this day and time to find such a caring, God-fearing company. My family, as always, support me in all I do. I was always told "can't never could." This book demonstrates that in a way I can never explain.

Hopefully my love of Mississippi, her restaurants, and her food, has been captured within these pages. I hope, too, that you will learn a little about each restaurant, make time to visit them when you can, and will try the recipes they shared with us. Eat the best; eat locally.

Love,

Anita Musgrove

Anita Musgrove, Author
STATE BACK ROAD RESTAURANTS COOKBOOK SERIES

"There is nothing better for a man, than that he should eat and drink, and that he should make his soul enjoy good in his labour. This also I saw, that it was from the hand of God."

Ecclesiastes 2:24

DELTA

Chatham
 Roy's Store 12

Clarksdale
 Hooker Grocer + Eatery 14
 Stone Pony Pizza 16

Cleveland
 J&W Smokehouse 18
 The Warehouse Deli 20

Greenville
 Scott's Hot Tamales 22

Greenwood
 The Crystal Grill 24

Indianola
 The Blue Biscuit 26
 The Crown Restaurant 28
 Nola Restaurant 30

Merigold
 Crawdad's Restaurant 32

Robinsonville
 The Hollywood Café 34

Rolling Fork
 Big Fella's 36

Yazoo City
 Café 7 38
 Christaphene's Bakery & Deli 40

Roy's Store

7 Roy's Store Road
Chatham, MS 38731
662-827-2588
www.royscabins.net
Find us on facebook

Roy's Store is located on beautiful Lake Washington right in the heart of the Delta where Pam Hammond has owned and operated the store for more then twenty years. Inside Roy's you will find a bait shop, groceries, and café. At Roy's, customers can enjoy a hot breakfast and a hearty lunch in the café while enjoying the view of the beautiful lake. Dinner is offered seasonally to accommodate hunters and anglers. Roy's invites all anglers, hunters, and vacationers to bunk in the lakeside cabins or camp in the primitive camping area and enjoy the beauty of the lake and surrounding areas.

Sunday: 6:00 am to 2:00 pm
Monday – Saturday: 6:00 am to 6:00 pm

Breakfast Biscuits

2 cups flour
1 tablespoon baking powder
1 teaspoon salt
½ teaspoon baking soda
½ cup cold butter, cubed
1 cup buttermilk

Preheat oven to 400°. Line a baking sheet with parchment paper or silicone baking mat. In a large bowl place flour, baking powder, salt and baking soda. Cut butter into flour mixture until it resembles coarse meal. Add buttermilk and stir to form dough. Drop dough in large spoonfuls on baking sheet. Bake until golden brown. Yields 16 biscuits.

Local Favorite

Banana Nut Bread

2 cups self-rising flour
2 cups sugar
2 sticks margarine, softened
2 teaspoons vanilla extract
3 eggs, beaten
3 ripe bananas, mashed
1 cup chopped nuts

Preheat oven to 350°. Mix all ingredients together. Pour into greased loaf pan. Bake 1 hour or until toothpick inserted in center comes out clean.

Local Favorite

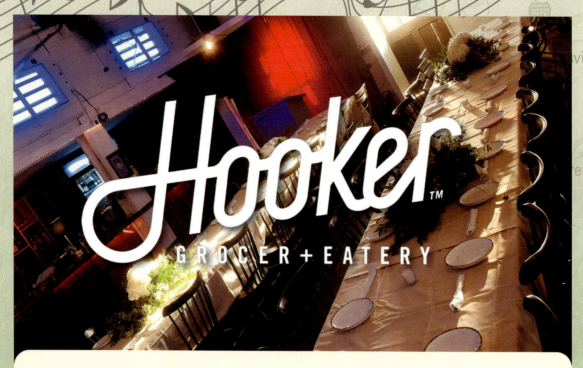

Hooker Grocer + Eatery

**316 John Lee Hooker Lane
Clarksdale, MS 38614
662-624-7038
www.hookergrocer.com
Find us on facebook**

Rooted firmly in the heart of the Mississippi Delta, Hooker Grocer + Eatery rubs elbows with some of Clarksdale's most iconic blues destinations, from the Delta Blues Museum and Ground Zero Blues Club to Red's and the Hambone Gallery. This humble eatery is a restaurant and bar with live music on selected nights. Visit for lunch or dinner to enjoy Southern atmosphere and tasty Southern classics like brisket sandwiches, smoked catfish dip, shrimp & grits, and so much more. Diners of an appropriate age may also try one of the house cocktails for an inspired taste of the Delta. Hooker Grocer + Eatery can't wait to serve you.

Wednesday – Saturday: 5:00 pm to 8:30 pm
Sunday: 11:00 am to 2:00 pm

Parmesan, Cheddar & Green Onion Biscuits

4 cups salted butter, cold
6 cups self-rising flour
1 tablespoon sugar
1 cup grated Parmesan cheese
1 cup shredded Cheddar cheese
½ cup chopped green onion
2 cups buttermilk
Melted butter for brushing

Preheat oven to 400°. In the bowl of a stand mixer fitted with a paddle attachment, combine butter, flour, sugar, cheeses and onion; mix on low speed until just combined. Change to dough hook attachment and add buttermilk; return to low speed. When dough comes together, transfer to a clean, floured surface and knead lightly. Form into a square. Using a rolling pin, roll out to about 2 inches thick. Cut with biscuit cutter and arrange biscuits on a greased baking sheet. Bake 12 to 15 minutes, remove from oven and brush biscuits with melted butter before serving.

Restaurant Recipe

Hooker Collard Greens

2 large onions, medium diced
1 pound carrots, medium diced
2 smoked ham hocks
6 quarts dried bonito stock
2 quarts chicken stock
½ cup packed brown sugar
Sambal hot chili sauce to taste
2 pounds smoked sausage, sliced into ¼-inch rounds
1 pound spicy souse
2 large bunches collard or turnip greens, chopped into medium to large pieces
10 sheets dried nori, cut into pieces

In a large stockpot, combine onion, carrot, ham hocks, bonito stock and chicken stock; bring to boil, then reduce heat and simmer 1 hour or until liquid is reduced by one-third. Add sugar and sambal; taste for desired seasoning and adjust as needed. Add sausage and souse, then cook at least 30 minutes or longer (longer cooking time will result in a more flavorful, full-bodied broth). Add greens and nori; simmer 1 hour or until both stems and leaves are tender. Enjoy.

Restaurant Recipe

Stone Pony Pizza

226 Delta Avenue
Clarksdale, MS 38614
662-624-7669
www.stoneponypizza.com
Find us on facebook

In June 2009, the idea of a gourmet pizza restaurant located in the heart of downtown Clarksdale was born. Owners and cousins Buddy Bass and Joe Weiss are fourth-generation Clarksdaleians who are proud of the history of Clarksdale and the new possibilities that await. With teenage, twenty-year-old, and thirty-year-old children of their own, Buddy and Joe had the goal to create a place where kids and families would feel comfortable dining and relaxing. They also wanted to create a restaurant at which visitors to Clarksdale could enjoy their time and experience local fare. Settle in at Stone Pony Pizza for pizza, salads, sandwiches, and so much more.

Monday – Thursday: 11:00 am to 10:00 pm
Friday & Saturday: 11:00 am to 11:00 pm

Twinkie Cake

15 Twinkies

½ cup sugar

1 (20-ounce) can crushed pineapple

1 (5.1-ounce) box instant vanilla pudding

2½ cups cold milk

4 bananas, sliced

1 (8-ounce) carton Cool Whip

¼ cup chopped pecans, optional

Maraschino cherries, optional

Line a 9x13-inch baking pan with Twinkies. Combine sugar and pineapple in a saucepan and bring to a boil; pour over Twinkies and set aside. In a bowl, combine pudding mix and milk; whisk 2 minutes until thickened. Arrange bananas over pineapple; top with pudding. Top with Cool Whip and, if desired, chopped pecans and cherries. Refrigerate at least 2 hours before serving.

Local Favorite

Tomato Dip

1 (8-ounce) package cream cheese, softened

1 (14-ounce) bottle ketchup

1 small onion, finely chopped

Dash hot sauce

In a bowl, beat cream cheese until smooth. Gradually blend in ketchup. Fold in onion and hot sauce. Refrigerate 24 hours before serving to allow flavors to develop. Serve with potato chips or corn chips.

Local Favorite

Delta

J & W Smokehouse

419 South Davis Avenue
Cleveland, MS 38732
662-579-8355
www.jandwsmokehouse.com
Find us on facebook

Conceived in 2009 by co-founders Kennedy Johnson, Jean Johnson, and Fitzgerald Watson, J & W Smokehouse came to be when Kennedy found one of his father's old rub recipes and used it to make a few slabs of ribs for his friends. They were so popular, he began cooking barbecue for cookouts, private parties, and other catered events. J & W Smokehouse was born. Today, the smokehouse provides smoked chicken, turkey, beef, and pork prepared the same way Kennedy's father did it more than 40 years ago. Come see why J & W Smokehouse is the Delta's best-kept barbecue secret.

Wednesday – Saturday: 11:00 am to 7:00 pm

Spaghetti

½ pound ground beef
½ cup chopped bell pepper
½ teaspoon salt
½ teaspoon black pepper
½ teaspoon garlic powder
½ teaspoon onion powder
1 (6-ounce) can tomato paste
1 tablespoon sugar
1 (16-ounce) package spaghetti

Brown beef with bell pepper. Add seasonings, tomato paste and sugar; mix well. Stir in 2 cups water. Simmer while cooking spaghetti. Bring 3 quarts salted water to a boil. Add spaghetti; cook to desired tenderness. Drain spaghetti and add to sauce. Mix well and serve.

Restaurant Recipe

Pecan Pie

3 eggs
1 cup sugar
½ cup white corn syrup
¾ stick margarine, melted
1 cup chopped pecans
1 (9-inch) unbaked pie shell

In a medium bowl, beat eggs. Blend in sugar. Stir in syrup, margarine, and pecans; mix well. Pour into pie shell and place in cold oven. Turn oven to 300°. Bake 1½ hours.

Restaurant Recipe

229 North Sharpe Avenue
Cleveland, MS 38732
662-846-7223
Find us on facebook

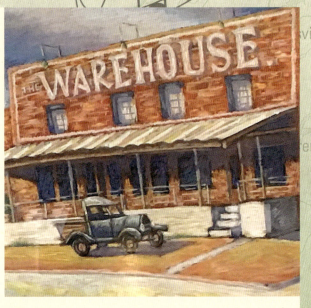

The Warehouse offers fine Southern dining rooted in Mississippi culture. Stop by any day of the week for their famous lunch featuring sandwiches, soups, and salads or buy wholesale cakes and meats. The Warehouse is a proud carrier of Boar's Head meats and cheeses; they guarantee your food is fresh and free of additives and hormones. Catering accommodations for special events can also be provided. Make The Warehouse your dining destination in Cleveland, Mississippi.

Sunday – Friday: 11:00 am to 2:00 pm
Saturday: 11:00 am to 3:00 pm

Barbecue Cups

1 pound ground chuck
½ cup barbecue sauce
2 tablespoons minced onion
1½ tablespoons brown sugar
1 (10-count) package refrigerator biscuits
¾ cup grated sharp Cheddar cheese

Preheat oven to 400°. Using a skillet over medium heat, brown meat until crumbly; drain. Stir in barbecue sauce, onion and sugar; cook 3 minutes. Grease a muffin pan with shortening and press each biscuit into the cups (you can stretch a 10-biscuit package into 12 cups). Spoon meat mixture into the cups and sprinkle with cheese. Bake 10 to 12 minutes or until brown

Local Favorite

Deconstructed Cabbage Rolls

1 tablespoon extra-virgin olive oil
1½ to 2 pounds lean ground beef
1 large onion, chopped
1 garlic clove, minced
1 small cabbage, chopped
2 (14-ounce) cans diced tomatoes
1 (8-ounce) can tomato sauce
1 teaspoon ground black pepper
1 teaspoon sea salt

In a large skillet, heat olive oil over medium heat. Add ground beef and onion; cook, stirring frequently and breaking up meat while stirring, until beef is no longer pink and onion is tender. Add garlic and continue cooking 1 minute. Add remaining ingredients and ½ cup water; bring to a boil. Cover and simmer 20 to 30 minutes, or until cabbage is tender.

Local Favorite

Scott's Hot Tamales

304 Martin Luther King Jr
Boulevard South
Greenville, MS 38701
662-332-4013
www.scottshottamales.com
Find us on facebook

Aaron and Elizabeth Scott started Scott's Hot Tamales in 1950, but the making of the tamales began many years earlier. Elizabeth's love for tamales prompted Aaron to get the recipe from a man of Mexican descent. Aaron believed it was better to make the tamales instead of repeatedly buying them. After a lot of tweaking, Aaron and Elizabeth developed the secret recipe, which still remains the same to this day. Scott's Hot Tamales has won various awards over the years in tamale competitions, but they're very proud of the "People's Choice" awards.

Tuesday – Saturday:
4:30 pm to 9:00 pm

Salisbury Steak

1 (10.75-ounce) can cream of mushroom soup, divided
1 pound ground beef
⅓ cup dry breadcrumbs
1 egg, beaten
¼ cup finely chopped onion
1 cup sliced mushrooms

Using a large bowl, thoroughly mix ¼ cup soup, meat, breadcrumbs, egg and onion; form into 6 patties. In a skillet over medium-high heat, brown patties on both sides. Remove patties, set aside and spoon off fat residue. Stir in remaining soup, ½ cup water and mushrooms. Return patties to skillet, reduce heat to low, cover and simmer 20 minutes while turning patties occasionally.

Restaurant Recipe

Tamale Delight

36 Nabisco Triscut Original Crackers
1 dozen Scott's hot tamales
1 (8-ounce) package shredded sharp cheese
1 (16-ounce) jar Pace picante sauce
1 (8-ounce) carton sour cream
1 bunch green onions, sliced
1 (8-ounce) can black olives, sliced
1 (12-ounce) jar sliced jalapeños

Preheat oven to 350°. Place crackers on baking sheet. Cut each tamale into 3 pieces, placing 1 piece on each cracker. Add ½ teaspoon cheese on top. Bake in oven 3 to 4 minutes or until cheese melts. Add ½ teaspoon picante sauce, and ½ teaspoon sour cream on top. Garnish with green onions, olives and jalapeños. Serve.

Restaurant Recipe

Hot Tamale and Cabbage Casserole

2 tablespoons olive oil
1 medium cabbage, cored, shredded and washed
1 tablespoon minced garlic
Salt and pepper to taste
2 dozen Scott's hot tamales
3 cups shredded Cheddar cheese, divided

Preheat oven to 375°. Heat oil in a large skillet over medium heat. Add cabbage and sauté, being careful not to overcook. Add garlic; cook 1 minute, stirring constantly. Season with salt and pepper. Using a 13x17-inch casserole dish, layer half the cabbage, all the hot tamales and 1½ cups cheese. Layer rest of cabbage and top with remaining cheese. Place in oven; heat until cheese melts.

Restaurant Recipe

423 Carrollton Avenue
Greenwood, MS 38930
662-453-6530
www.crystalgrillms.com
Find us on facebook

On your next drive through the Mississippi Delta, stop by The Crystal Grill, a Greenwood gem renowned for its wide array of menu choices. Serving everything from seafood to pasta and steak to sandwiches, the restaurant has something to satisfy everyone's taste buds. The Crystal Grill makes everything from scratch with fresh ingredients, so you can enjoy a great-tasting meal every visit. The menu even features vegetarian and gluten-free options to accommodate guests with specific dietary needs. Whatever you decide to eat, just be sure to save room for dessert. The lemon icebox pie comes highly recommended. Visit The Crystal Grill for Southern food done right.

Thursday – Sunday: 11:00 am to 8:00 pm

Pink Velvet Salad

This is the most popular summer salad on the menu. Served with summer fruit, melons and grapes.

1 cup cherry pie filling
1 cup crushed pineapple, drained
1 (14-ounce) can sweetened condensed milk
Dash lemon juice
Dash salt
Dash almond flavoring
¼ cup chopped pecans
4 ounces Cool Whip

Thoroughly mix all ingredients, except Cool Whip. Fold in Cool Whip. Line a loaf pan with foil. Pour mixture into pan and freeze. When frozen solid, lift out of pan and wrap again for storage in freezer. Slice and serve on hot summer days.

Restaurant Recipe

501 Second Street
Indianola, MS 38751
662-645-0258
www.thebluebiscuit.com
Find us on facebook

Opened in 2010, The Blue Biscuit serves up the Delta's best Southern classics in a circa 1940s storefront. Located across from the B.B. King Museum, this Delta favorite offers an exciting menu, featuring seventy-two hours smoked pulled pork, fried catfish, hushpuppies, burgers, and old-fashioned soul food lunches. Visitors come for the delicious food and drink and stay for the Delta's best live music. A popular haunt for locals as well as international business and blues travelers, The Blue Biscuit is the place to be to experience the best blues, barbecue, and cold brews that the Delta has to offer. Come get your biscuits buttered

LUNCH:
Monday, Friday & Saturday: 11:00 am to 2:00 pm
DINNER:
Friday: 4:00 pm to 11:00 pm
Saturday: 5:00 pm to 12:30 am
Sunday: 5:00 pm to 10:00 pm

Corned Beef Hash Frittata

1 pound small red potatoes scrubbed and cut into ½-inch cubes
1½ teaspoons salt
¾ teaspoon pepper
10 large eggs
3 tablespoons heavy cream
1 tablespoon spicy brown mustard
1 tablespoon vegetable oil
1 medium onion, diced
½ pound deli corned beef, diced
2 tablespoons chopped chives

Preheat oven to 400°. Place potatoes in a microwave-safe bowl with salt and pepper; stir. Cover bowl with plastic wrap; microwave on high 6 minutes or until fork-tender. Whisk together, eggs, cream and mustard. Heat oil in cast-iron skillet over medium heat until oil begins to shimmer. Add onion; cook until tender and translucent. Add potatoes and corned beef. Pour egg mixture over top and using a spatula make sure mixture surrounds the onions and corned beef. Cook on top of stove 1 minute, then transfer to oven. Bake 12 to 14 minutes or until the eggs are fully set. Top with chives and serve.

Local Favorite

Mississippi Baked Corn

1 tablespoon butter
2 tablespoons flour
1 cup milk
1 (15-ounce) can whole-kernel corn
2 teaspoons sugar
1 teaspoon salt
Dash paprika
2 eggs, separated

In a skillet, melt butter; stir in flour to make roux. Add milk; bring to a boil. Add corn, sugar, salt, paprika and egg yolks. Continue to cook about 30 minutes, stirring often to prevent sticking. Beat egg whites until they form soft peaks. Remove corn from heat; fold in egg whites. Pour in buttered, 8-inch square casserole dish. Bake at 350° for 30 minutes.

Local Favorite

The Crown Restaurant

112 Front Avenue
Indianola, MS 38751
662-887-4522
www.thecrownrestaurant.com
Find us on facebook

When you visit The Crown Restaurant, make sure you're starving because this Indianola mainstay serves up real Southern hospitality that is guaranteed to fill you up. Since 1976, The Crown has catered to the appetites of generations of Mississippians, offering its own spin on old favorites. From salads to specials that change weekly, The Crown has it all. After you've eaten, browse original Delta art, peruse the gift shop for classic children's toys and gifts, or pick up a Taste of Gourmet box mix or sauce to enjoy a taste of The Crown at home. Visit The Crown Restaurant and eat like a king

GIFT SHOP:
Tuesday – Saturday: 9:00 am to 5:00 pm
RESTAURANT:
Tuesday – Saturday: 11:00 am to 2:00 pm

Magnolia Macaroon Pie

1 stick unsalted butter
1½ cups sugar
¼ cup all-purpose flour
¼ teaspoon salt
2 eggs, beaten
1⅓ cups flaked coconut
¼ cup chopped pecans
(or almonds), optional
1 (9-inch) frozen pie crust, thawed

Preheat oven to 325°. In a saucepan over low heat, melt butter. Stir in sugar, flour, salt and ½ cup water, combining well. Add eggs and coconut, mixing thoroughly. Scatter pecans in bottom of pie crust, then pour filling into crust. Bake 45 minutes.

Restaurant Recipe

The Crown's Fresh Broccoli Salad

This Broccoli Salad is best made the day before you plan to serve it.

6 cups coarsely chopped broccoli florets
1 cup green or black olives, chopped
½ cup finely chopped onion
1 cup mayonnaise
¼ cup olive juice
⅓ cup sugar
Salt and pepper to taste

In a large bowl, mix all ingredients together, tossing to combine. Taste and adjust seasoning, if needed. Stir before serving.

Restaurant Recipe

Chicken Allison

6 boneless, skinless chicken breasts
½ teaspoon salt
½ teaspoon black pepper
1 lemon, sliced

To a large skillet, add chicken, salt, pepper and lemon. Cover with water and bring to a light simmer. Poach chicken 4 to 5 minutes; gently lift from water and set aside to drain.

Allison Butter:

1 cup grated Parmesan cheese
1 stick butter, softened
6 tablespoons mayonnaise
½ teaspoon Worcestershire sauce
½ teaspoon Tabasco sauce
6 green onions, finely chopped

In a mixing bowl, combine all ingredients except onions; blend with a hand mixer. Gently fold in onions. Place chicken breasts on a baking sheet; cover each with 2 tablespoons Allison Butter. Broil until deeply browned. Serve over rice, topped with juices released during baking. Serves 6.

Restaurant Recipe

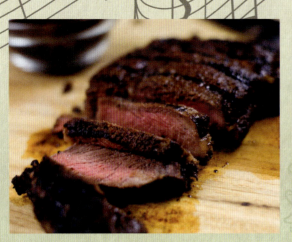

Nola Restaurant

112 Court Avenue
Indianola, MS 38751
662-887-2990
www.nolainthedelta.com
Find us on facebook and Instagram

Nola is a true Southern restaurant serving the community of downtown Indianola. The restaurant prides itself on using ingredients of the best quality available to create simple yet unique Southern cuisine for all to enjoy. The varied menu features salads, steaks, seafood, and pasta dishes. Nola also offers special entrées and desserts that change by the day. Visit the team at Nola for a specialty drink from the bar and a delicious meal from their kitchen.

Tuesday – Saturday: 5:00 pm to 9:00 pm
CALL FOR RESERVATIONS

Crawfish Dirty Rice

Rice
1 red bell pepper, diced
Olive oil
1 link Cajun sausage, diced
2 large shallots, minced
3 garlic cloves, minced
Salt and pepper to taste
1 teaspoon paprika
2 teaspoons thyme
White wine, for deglazing
2 pounds Louisiana crawfish tails
1 teaspoon Worcestershire sauce

Cook rice and set aside. In a large pot over medium heat, sauté bell pepper in olive oil until tender. Add sausage, shallots and garlic. Season with salt, pepper, paprika and thyme; cook until sausage is heated through. Deglaze pot with white wine. Add crawfish and Worcestershire. Cook 5 to 7 minutes; toss in rice mixing well.

Restaurant Recipe

Grits and Grillades

Bacon
1 onion, diced
4 jalapenos, deseeded and diced
2 celery stalks, diced
3 garlic cloves, minced
1 tomato, diced
1 (15-ounce) can beef broth
Thyme to taste
Paprika to taste
Round steak, cut into 4 portions
Salt and pepper
Flour for dredging
Oil for frying
2 ounces red wine
Grits, cooked
8 green onions, thinly sliced
(for garnish)

In a Dutch oven over medium heat, render bacon until crisp; remove, leaving 2 tablespoons fat in bottom. Sauté onion, jalapenos and celery until tender. Add garlic and tomato; sauté 5 minutes. Add broth, thyme and paprika; simmer while cooking steak. Season steak with salt and pepper, dredge in flour and brown well in skillet with oil. Remove steaks and deglaze skillet with wine; add to Dutch oven. Add steak, bring to a boil and allow to thicken. Serve over cooked grits. Top with green onions and crumbled bacon.

Restaurant Recipe

Crawdad's
RESTAURANT

104 North Park Street
Merigold, MS 38759
662-748-2441
www.crawdadsms.com
Find us on facebook

In 1984, Crawdad's opened on Old Highway 61, serving crawfish out of a small six-seater building. The location was so small, the crawfish had to be cooked on the porch due to lack of room. One complete building move, fourteen renovations, and thirty-five years later, Crawdad's is still going, a milestone few other restaurants in the Delta have achieved. Crawdad's still serves crawfish, but over the years, the menu has expanded to include a range of other items, from fried mushrooms and grilled oysters to grilled steaks and black bottom pie. Stop by this Delta mainstay for a taste of the "Crawdad's Life."

Tuesday – Thursday: 5:00 pm to 9:00 pm
Friday & Saturday: 5:00 pm to 10:00 pm

Deviled Crab

⅓ cup vinegar
3 eggs, lightly beaten
1 tablespoon Worcestershire sauce
1 tablespoon butter, melted
1 teaspoon mustard
½ teaspoon celery seed
Salt and pepper to taste
1 tablespoon flour
1 cup fresh crabmeat in shells (reserve shells)
1 cup crushed crackers

Preheat oven to 400°. In a saucepan over low heat, mix ⅔ cup water and vinegar; mix in eggs. In a small bowl, mix Worcestershire, butter and mustard; add to saucepan. Add celery seed, salt and pepper. Cook 3 minutes, stirring often. In a small bowl, mix flour with 1 teaspoon water; add to saucepan and cook until mixture thickens. Remove from heat; fold in crabmeat and crackers. Spoon into shells. Bake 15 to 20 minutes, or until heated through. Serves 6.

Local Favorite

Old School Burgers

2 slices bread, finely crumbled
1 small onion, minced
1 pound ground beef
¾ teaspoon salt
Pepper to taste

In a medium bowl, mix bread with ¼ cup water. Add onion, beef, salt and pepper, mixing well with hands. Shape into 4 patties. Cook about 10 minutes in greased frying pan over medium heat, turning once to brown both sides.

Local Favorite

The Hollywood Café

1585 Old Commerce Road
Robinsonville, MS 38664
662-363-1225
www.thehollywoodcafe.com
Find us on facebook

The Hollywood Café offers a unique taste of the traditional Mississippi Delta, untainted by time. Customers enjoy Southern delicacies such as catfish, hushpuppies, and possibly the best hamburger ever to be served. The café is also home of the fried pickle, invented by a former cook who dipped pickle slices in catfish batter and deep-fried them. In addition to the great food, The Hollywood Café is famously immortalized in Marc Cohn's song "Walking in Memphis," who was inspired after performing at the café with gospel singer and pianist Muriel Wilkins. A part of the Mississippi Blues Trail, The Hollywood Café provides both tasty food and rich history.

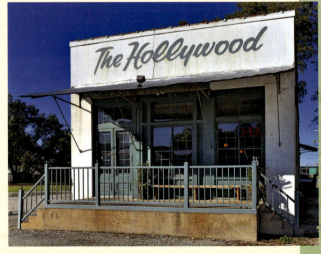

Monday – Thursday: 10:00 am to 9:00 pm
Friday & Saturday: 10:00 am to 10:00 pm

Buttermilk Pie

3 cups sugar

6 tablespoons all-purpose flour

1½ cups buttermilk, divided

5 eggs

½ cup (1 stick) melted butter

2 teaspoons vanilla extract

2 (9-inch) pie crusts, unbaked

1 cup chopped pecans, optional

Preheat oven to 425°. In a bowl, combine sugar, flour and ¾ cup buttermilk. Add eggs and remaining buttermilk; mix well. Stir in butter and vanilla, then divide mixture between pie crusts. Top with pecans, if desired. Bake 10 minutes; reduce heat to 350° and bake 25 to 30 minutes longer or until a knife inserted into the center comes out clean. Cool completely and store in the refrigerator.

Family Favorite

Slow-Cooker Mississippi Pot Roast

2 tablespoons olive oil (or vegetable oil)

1 (3-pound) chuck roast

Salt and pepper to taste

1 (1-ounce) packet ranch dressing mix

1 (1-ounce) packet onion soup mix

1 stick butter

8 pepperoncini peppers

To a large skillet over high heat, add oil. Pat both sides of roast dry with paper towels; season with salt and pepper. Add roast to skillet and sear until golden brown, about 2 to 3 minutes on each side; transfer to slow cooker. Add dry mixes to slow cooker along with butter and pepperoncini. Set to low heat and cook at least 8 hours. Using 2 forks, shred meat, discarding any fatty pieces. Serve.

Family Favorite

34178 Mississippi 1
Rolling Fork, MS 39159
662-873-9356
Find us on facebook

Nestled in the heart of the Delta is this lost treasure, Big Fella's Restaurant. The owner, Marty Long, is a barbeque competitor who participates in competitions all over the United States. When he's not competing, he's cooking up delicious hand-cut steaks, ribs, pork chops, shish kabobs, and specialty burgers. In addition, he offers some great shrimp and catfish dishes. Not only does Big Fella's offer great food, they also sell locally produced goods like honey and seasonings. Do not pass by Big Fella's, it will be your loss. Good food and friendly service.

Thursday: 5:00 pm to 9:00 pm
Friday: 10:00 am to 2:00 pm
5:00 pm to 10:00 pm
Saturday: 5:00 pm to 10:00 pm
Sunday: 11:00 am to 2:00 pm

Mustard Fried Fish

Oil for frying
5 ounces Louisiana hot sauce (if you want hotter use Tabasco)
8 ounces yellow mustard
Fish fillets
Louisiana lemon-flavor fish breading

Using a deep fat fryer, heat oil to 350°. In a large bowl, mix hot sauce and mustard well. Add fish fillets; stir and toss to evenly coat fish. Bread fish. Deep-fry until golden brown.

Restaurant Recipe

Crabmeat Cream Sauce

4 cups heavy cream
1 stick salted butter
Pinch kosher salt
Pinch black pepper
1 teaspoon Old Bay seasoning
½ cup cooked blue crab claw meat
4 teaspoons Parmesan cheese
1 teaspoon chopped parsley

In a saucepan over medium-low heat, cook all ingredients, stirring frequently, until hot. Spoon over steaks or other meat of choice.

Restaurant Recipe

Loaded Baked Beans

1 (114-ounce) can Showboat pork and beans
2 bell peppers, diced
1 sweet onion, diced
1 red onion, diced
2 pounds pork sausage, browned and drained
1 cup vinegar
4 cups Kraft barbecue sauce
2 cups brown sugar
¼ cup Big Fella's Seasoning
4 teaspoons Montreal steak seasoning
Salt and pepper to taste

Preheat oven to 400°. Mix all ingredients together in a large aluminum pan; cover tightly with foil. Bake 45 minutes; remove foil. Cook an additional 10 minutes uncovered. Remove from oven and enjoy.

Restaurant Recipe

Café 7

1527 Jerry Clower Boulevard
Yazoo City, MS 39194
662-746-8666
Find us on facebook

Café 7 got its start in April of 2012. The cooks at Café 7 spent many hours in the kitchen of Yazoo's famous, "The Steak House," until it closed. Southern favorites from chitterlings to smothered pork chops and turnip greens to frog legs can be found on the menu. Don't forget to ask about their daily specials. Café 7 has developed a loyal following in the time since it has opened so be sure to stop by for some great Southern cooking while you are in Yazoo.

Tuesday – Thursday: 11:00 am to 2:00 pm, 5:00 pm to 9:00 pm
Friday: 11:00 am to 2:00 pm, 5:00 pm to 10:00 pm
Saturday: 5:00 pm to 10:00 pm

Butter Fingers

1½ sticks butter, softened

¼ cup sugar

2 teaspoons vanilla

1 cup ground black walnuts

2 cups all-purpose flour, sifted twice

Dash salt

Powdered sugar for dusting tops

Preheat oven to 300°. Using an electric mixer, cream together butter and sugar. Add vanilla and nuts; mix well. Add 2 teaspoons ice-cold water, flour and salt; mix well. Remove mixture from bowl and knead thoroughly on lightly floured surface. Roll dough into a log about the thickness of a finger; slice into 1-inch-long sections and place on a parchment-lined cookie sheet. Bake 30 minutes or until light brown. When cookies have cooled completely, dust with powdered sugar. Store in an air-tight container lined with wax paper. Butter Fingers keep a long time and the flavor improves with age.

Local Favorite

Shrimp Delight

2 pounds boiled shrimp

5 cups cooked small elbow macaroni

6 hard-boiled eggs, chopped

1 small onion, finely chopped

1 cup mayonnaise

Dash garlic powder

Salt and pepper to taste

6 lettuce leaves

2 ripe tomatoes, cut in wedges

Combine shrimp, macaroni, eggs, onion, mayonnaise, garlic powder, salt and pepper. Taste and adjust seasoning to taste. Plate with a lettuce leaf, heaping spoon shrimp mixture and tomato wedge.

Local Favorite

Christaphene's Bakery & Deli

408 North Jerry Clower Boulevard
Yazoo City, MS 39194
662-590-7138
Find us on facebook

Established in December 2015, Christaphene's Bakery & Deli was opened by Susan Porter, a small-town girl following a big dream. In addition to a bakery offering homemade breads, casseroles, and desserts, the deli side of Christaphene's offers delicious sandwiches and freshly made salads. Stop by for a tasty lunch and take home a sweet treat when you leave. From cakes to cookies to cinnamon rolls, Christaphene's Bakery & Deli has it all.

Tuesday – Friday:
10:00 am to 5:00 pm

Four-Layer Dessert

First Layer:

1 cup all-purpose flour

1 stick melted butter

½ cup chopped pecans

Preheat oven to 350°. Combine all ingredients and press into 9x13-inch pan. Bake 20 minutes; cool.

Second Layer:

1 (8-ounce) package cream cheese, softened

1 cup powdered sugar

1 (12-ounce) container Cool Whip, divided

Blend cream cheese, powdered sugar and 1 cup Cool Whip. Spread over cooled first layer.

Third Layer:

2 (3.9-ounce) boxes instant chocolate pudding mix

3 cups cold milk

Beat 2 minutes or until thick; pour over second layer.

Fourth Layer:

Spread remaining Cool Whip over third layer and garnish with shaved chocolate bark.

Family Favorite

Hot Cocoa

2 cups powdered sugar

1 cup cocoa

2½ cups powdered milk

1 teaspoon salt

Pinch cayenne pepper, or to taste

Combine all ingredients in a resealable container. Fill mug half full of cocoa mix and add 4 to 6 ounces hot water or milk.

Restaurant Recipe

Cake Mix Cookies

1 box butter recipe cake mix

⅓ cup vegetable oil

2 eggs

Preheat oven to 350°. In a mixing bowl, combine all ingredients until well mixed. Scoop onto lightly greased baking pan and bake 10 to 12 minutes, or until golden brown.

Restaurant Recipe

HILLS

Batesville
Dixieland BBQ 44

Booneville
Market 105 46

Como
The Como Steakhouse 48

Corinth
Pizza Grocery 50

Fulton
Theo's Feed Mill 52

Grenada
333 Restaurant 54

Hernando
Bazar's Bakery & Breakfast 56

Holly Springs
Annie's Home Cooking 58
Marshall Steakhouse 60
Phillips Grocery 62

Oxford
Ajax Diner 64
The Beacon Restaurant 66
Boure Restaurant 68

Tupelo
Bar-B-Q by Jim 70
Connie's Fried Chicken 72
Crossroads Rib Shack 74
Neon Pig 76
Romie's Grocery 78
Sweet Tea & Biscuits Café 80

Author Anita as a child with her sister.

Dixieland BBQ

128 Highway 51 North
Batesville, MS 38606
662-563-2271
Find us on facebook

Dixieland BBQ is a family-owned and family-operated business in Batesville offering outstanding barbecue plus hot fresh-made pork skins and their ever-popular chess pie squares for dessert. Call on Dixieland BBQ for your catering needs and your next event is sure to be a success. For your next family gathering, order crowd-pleasing sausage and cheese platters. Next time you are in the Batesville area, stop at Dixieland for a terrific meal and get your souvenir T-shirt while there.

Monday – Thursday: 10:30 am to 7:00 pm
Friday: 10:30 am to 8:00 pm
Saturday: 10:30 am to 6:00 pm

Holiday Punch

1 cup sugar
1 teaspoon whole cloves
3 sticks cinnamon
2 quarts orange juice
1 quart cranberry juice cocktail
¼ cup lemon juice
Lemon (or orange) slices for garnish

Pour 1 cup water in a large saucepan over low heat. Add sugar, cloves and cinnamon; simmer 15 minutes. Remove and discard cloves and cinnamon sticks. Add juices and continue to cook until hot (but do not boil). Serve hot with lemon or orange slices floating on top.

Local Favorite

Shrimp Pie

1 sleeve saltine crackers, crumbled
4 cups boiled, peeled and deveined shrimp
1 stick butter, sliced
3 cups milk
2 tablespoons Worcestershire sauce
1 egg, beaten
1 teaspoon mustard
Salt and pepper to taste
3 tablespoons ketchup
½ tablespoon hot sauce

Preheat oven to 400°. In a 1-quart casserole dish, place a layer of cracker crumbs, then a layer of shrimp; dot with butter. Repeat layers until dish is full. Mix remaining ingredients in a bowl; pour over shrimp and cracker crumbs. Bake 30 minutes or until set.

Local Favorite

MARKET 105

105 West College Street
Booneville, MS 38829
662-720-6304
www.market105booneville.com
Find us on facebook

Welcome to The Market. Established in 2017, Market 105 opened with the goal to enrich the lives of all guests that enter its doors. The restaurant fosters an all-in-one environment where anyone can eat, shop, and gather. The menu features classic appetizers, savory sandwiches, refreshing salads, and a rotating blue plate special. Market 105 also offers build-your-own pizzas, specialty pizzas, pastas, and keto-friendly dishes for diners with specific dietary needs. Visit Market 105 today and get ready to eat

Monday – Friday: 11:00 am to 6:00 pm
Saturday: 8:00 am to 3:00 pm

Bread Pudding with Irish Cream Sauce

6 ro 8 large croissants
11 eggs, beaten
1⅓ cups sugar
4 cups milk
1 teaspoon vanilla extract
½ teaspoon ground cinnamon

Preheat oven to 375°. Cut croissants into 1-inch pieces and place into a greased 9x13-inch baking dish. In a mixing bowl, combine eggs, sugar, milk, vanilla and cinnamon; pour over croissant pieces and let sit at least 20 minutes (or overnight in refrigerator). Bake 40 to 45 minutes or until set.

Irish Cream Sauce:

1 stick butter
1 cup packed brown sugar
½ cup heavy cream
Irish cream liquer to taste

In a saucepan, combine butter and sugar; bring to a boil, stirring often. Add heavy cream and return to a boil. Add Irish cream and stir. Remove from heat, cool slightly and pour over Bread Pudding.

Restaurant Recipe

Chicken & Dumplings

2 pounds chicken
1 teaspoon salt
1 teaspoon black pepper
¼ cup shortening
2 teaspoons bacon grease
3 cups self-rising flour
1 cup milk
¼ cup (½ stick) butter
¼ cup half-and-half

To a large pot, add chicken; cover with water and bring to a boil. Reduce to a simmer and cook 20 to 30 minutes or until chicken is cooked through. Reserving broth, remove chicken, then cool and chop; set aside. Add salt and pepper to broth and return to a boil. In a bowl, cut shortening and bacon grease into flour, mixing until crumbly. Add milk and stir until moistened. Turn dough out onto a lightly floured surface and roll out to ⅛-inch thickness; cut into 1-inch pieces. When broth comes to a boil, add butter and half-and-half, then add dumplings a few at a time, stirring gently. Reduce to simmer and cook, stirring often, 25 minutes. Return chicken to pot just until heated through and serve.

Restaurant Recipe

The Como Steakhouse

203 Main Street
Como, MS 38619
662-526-9529
Find us on facebook

First opened in 1988, The Como Steakhouse became a North Mississippi staple by serving its famous hickory-charcoaled steaks to locals and travelers alike. At The Como Steakhouse, it's not unusual to encounter a line of patrons waiting to be seated, but the wait is worth it. The juicy steaks are aged twenty-seven days, cut by hand, and grilled to perfection atop a charcoal-fired, open-pit grill. Patrons also flock to the steakhouse for its atmosphere. Housed inside a 125-year-old former mercantile store, the steakhouse harks back to small-town Mississippi of days past. A sense of nostalgia coupled with unmatched fare await all who visit The Como Steakhouse.

Monday – Thursday: 5:00 pm to 10:00 pm
Friday & Saturday: 4:30 pm to 10:00 pm

Como Delight

Cookie crumb crust
Prepared chocolate pudding
Cream cheese, softened
Whipped cream for topping
Pecans, toasted and chopped

In a 9x13-inch baking dish, bake cookie crumb crust at 375° until golden brown; cool completely. In a bowl, blend together chocolate pudding and cream cheese until smooth; spread in even layer over crust. Top with an even layer of whipped cream. Sprinkle with pecans, cover with foil and refrigerate several hours before serving.

Restaurant Recipe

Sausage & Cheese Plate

1 link smoked sausage, deep-fried
Pepperoncinis
Pepper Jack cheese, cubed
Cheddar cheese, cubed
Homemade ranch dressing for dipping
Como House special seasoning for sprinkling

Slice sausage into rounds and plate along with pepperoncinis, cheeses and a sauce cup of ranch. Sprinkle entire plate with seasoning and serve while sausage is hot.

Restaurant Recipe

800 Cruise Street
Corinth, MS 38834
662-287-3200
www.pizzagrocery.com
Find us on facebook

Since 2006, Pizza Grocery has been "the crossroads for great food and friendly service." Located in historic downtown Corinth, the restaurant quickly became a local favorite. More than a decade later, Pizza Grocery is still an excellent spot for social gatherings. The chef prepares a diverse menu that is ideal for dining with family and friends, and the carefully crafted weekend specials offer guests fine dining in a casual atmosphere that is perfect for date nights. Pizza Grocery provides the right atmosphere for catching up with friends, watching the game, or impressing that special someone. Come taste the flavor of Italy with Southern hospitality.

LUNCH:
Monday – Saturday: 11:00 am to 2:00 pm
DINNER:
Monday – Thursday: 5:00 pm to 8:00 pm
Friday & Saturday: 5:00 pm to 9:00 pm

Pimento Cheese Fritters

Prepared (or store-bought) pimento cheese
Flour for dredging
2 eggs, beaten
Panko breadcrumbs for dredging

Preheat deep fryer to 350°. Roll 1½-ounce portions of pimento cheese into balls. Dredge in flour, dip in egg wash and roll in panko to coat. Fry until golden brown.

Restaurant Recipe

Meatballs

10 pounds ground beef
1 yellow onion, diced
6 leaves basil, chopped
2 cups grated Parmesan cheese
2 cups Italian-style breadcrumbs
3 eggs, slightly beaten
Salt and pepper to taste

Preheat oven to 400°. In a large bowl, mix all ingredients until thoroughly combined. Roll into 3-ounce balls and arrange on a baking sheet; bake 1 to 1½ hours until browned and juices run clear.

Restaurant Recipe

Theo's Feed Mill

400 South Spring Street
Fulton, MS 38843
662-862-4994
Find us on facebook

Theo's Feed Mill opened in 2018 when owner Matt Moore combined his passion for catering with a desire to resurrect the old feed mill building in Fulton. His family-friendly restaurant serves Matt's locally famous barbecue and has also allowed him to expand the menu to include more favorites likes Brashear's Boudin Bites, Petit's Mississippi Rattlesnake Eggs, and Brown's "Howlin' at the Moonshine" Tacos. Check out their daily lunch specials for unique dishes that are sure to please. Don't miss a stop in Fulton to enjoy the historical building, a fun and cozy atmosphere, and a super delicious meal.

LUNCH:
Sunday – Friday: 11:00 am to 2:00 pm
DINNER:
Thursday – Saturday: 5:00 pm to 11:00 pm

Dutch Baby

2 large eggs
½ cup flour
½ cup milk
Pinch of salt
4 tablespoons butter
1 lemon
Powdered sugar for garnish
Fresh berries, optional

Place a 9- or 10-inch cast-iron skillet in oven and preheat to 450°. Using a mixing bowl, whisk together eggs, flour, milk and salt, beating well. Carefully remove skillet from oven, add butter and swirl the pan to coat. Immediately add batter to pan and return to oven. Bake 12 to 15 minutes or until pancake is puffed and golden brown. Remove from oven, squeeze the lemon over pancake and dust with powdered sugar. Serve immediately with berries, if desired.

Local Favorite

Roasted Root Vegetables

4 large carrots, peeled and cut into 1-inch cubes
2 medium potatoes, peeled and cut into 1-inch cubes
2 medium sweet potatoes, peeled and cut into 1-inch cubes
3 medium beets, peeled and cut into 1-inch cubes
4 small onions, peeled and cut in half
1 garlic bulb, cloves separated, peeled and left whole
3 tablespoons olive oil
2 teaspoons salt
1 teaspoon pepper

Preheat oven to 400°. Add vegetables to large cast-iron skillet. Drizzle with olive oil. Sprinkle with salt and pepper, toss to coat. Bake 45 minutes, stirring every 15 minutes, until vegetables are tender.

Local Favorite

333 Restaurant

515 Scenic Loop 333
Grenada, MS 38901
662-229-0020
Find us on facebook

333 Restaurant, at the main entrance to Grenada Lake, is a local full-service, dine-in, family-owned favorite that has been in business since 2005. They have been voted Best Steak, Best Seafood/Crawfish, and Best Family Restaurant six years in a row by the local Grenada Star Newspaper readers. 333 caters reunions and events, feeds ball teams and birthday parties in their large dining rooms, private back dining room, and outdoor patio/bar complete with stage. Their specialty is Southern soul food hot plates, charcoal-grilled steaks, boiled crawfish, seafood, and catfish entrées. Online ordering, curbside delivery, take outs, and a self-serve kiosk order entry are available. 333 supports the local soup kitchen and charities.

Sunday – Wednesday: 11:00 am to 3:00 pm
Thursday– Saturday: 11:00 am to 9:00 pm

Mississippi BACK ROAD RESTAURANT Recipes

333 House-Made Ranch Salad Dressing

1 gallon mayonnaise

4 tablespoons finely chopped dried chives

2 tablespoons dried dill

4 tablespoons finely chopped dried parsley

4 tablespoons garlic powder

4 tablespoons onion powder

2 tablespoons salt

2 tablespoons fine-ground pepper

1 gallon fat-free buttermilk

In a large stainless steel bowl, whisk together mayonnaise and all dry seasonings. Slowly whisk in buttermilk until smooth. Refrigerate 2 hours before serving on salads and as appetizer dip.

Restaurant Recipes

333 1000 Island Dressing

1 gallon mayonnaise

4 tablespoons onion powder

2 tablespoons paprika

2 tablespoons salt

2 tablespoons fresh-squeezed lemon juice

¼ cup Worcestershire sauce

½ cup green olive juice

½ cup sweet pickle relish

2 cups ketchup

In a large stainless steel mixing bowl, whisk together mayonnaise and all dry seasonings. Slowly whisk in wet ingredients until smooth. Refrigerate dressing immediately. For best flavor, chill 2 hours before serving on salads and as appetizer dip.

333 Comeback Sauce:

½ teaspoon horseradish

¼ cup 1000 Island Dressing

In a small bowl, stir together horseradish and 1000 Island. Serve chilled with 333 Fried Green Tomatoes and 333 Hand-Battered Fried Onion Rings.

Restaurant Recipe

Bazar's Bakery & Breakfast

210 East Commerce Street
Hernando, MS 38632
662-288-1600
Find us on facebook

Bazar's Bakery & Breakfast is a hometown bakery and restaurant built to serve all your fresh-baked needs. From cupcakes and cakes to full-service breakfast, brunch, and lunch, Bazar's does it all. The restaurant serves up savory items like soups, quiche, patty melts, wings, and even steaks. Not to be overshadowed, the bakery offers dozens of baked desserts to sate your sweet tooth. Enjoy cupcakes, cookies, custom cakes, keto desserts, sugar-free desserts, gluten-free desserts, and so much more. No matter what your fix is, Bazar's Bakery & Breakfast has it

Monday – Friday: 8:00 am to 5:00 pm
Saturday & Sunday: 8:00 am to 2:00 pm

Spicy Avocado Toast

1 slice white bread
1 avocado, pitted and peeled
1 teaspoon each salt and pepper
½ teaspoon red chili flakes
2 slices tomato
1 egg, fried
1 cup sour cream
2 tablespoons fresh lime juice
1 tablespoon dried dill

Toast bread as desired. In a bowl, mash together avocado, salt, pepper and chili flakes; spread evenly on toast. Top toast with tomato slices, then with egg. In a bowl, whisk together sour cream, lime juice and dill; drizzle over toast. Enjoy.

Restaurant Recipe

Keto Chicken Lime Soup

1 tablespoon olive oil
1 cup minced red onion
2 jalapeños, minced
2 cloves garlic, minced
7 cups chicken stock
2 tomatoes, deseeded and diced
½ teaspoon ground cumin
2 pounds boneless chicken breasts
5 tablespoons fresh lime juice
Salt and pepper to taste
¼ cup chopped fresh cilantro
1 avocado, pitted, peeled and sliced
Corn tortillas, cut into strips and fried crisp

To a stockpot over medium-low heat, add oil, onion, peppers and garlic; sauté 3 minutes. Add stock, tomatoes, cumin and chicken. Bring to a boil and reduce to a simmer for 20 minutes or until chicken is cooked through. Remove chicken and cool; chop and return to soup. Add lime juice, salt and pepper; cook 5 more minutes. Serve soup with a garnish of cilantro, avocado and tortilla strips.

Restaurant Recipe

Annie's Home Cooking

200 North Memphis Street
Holly Springs, MS 38635
662-252-4222
Find us on facebook

Annie's Home Cooking serves up home-style cooking in the heart of Holly Springs. Join Annie for a meal, whether you're eating at the restaurant, picking up take-out, or having it delivered. Annie's takes pleasure in providing guests with warm Southern hospitality and tasty soulful cooking just like mama used to make. Be sure to try the famous fried chicken as well as a range of homemade sides, from okra to cornbread. Come on by for a taste of Miss Annie's home cooking.

Monday – Wednesday: 11:00 am to 3:00 pm
Thursday – Saturday: 11:00 am to 9:00 pm
Sunday: 11:00 am to 4:30 pm

Baked Apples

4 medium cooking apples
⅓ cup sugar
¼ teaspoon cinnamon
1 tablespoon margarine, quartered

Preheat oven to 350°. Core apples about three quarters of the way, leaving a little in the bottom. Place apples in baking pan. Mix sugar and cinnamon; fill centers of apples. Place 1 margarine quarter on top of filling in each apple. Pour ½ cup water in bottom of pan. Bake 45 minutes or until apples are tender. If apples seem dry while cooking, spoon liquid from bottom of pan over top of apples.

Local Favorite

Cornbread Salad

1 (8.5-ounce) package cornbread mix
½ cup milk
1 large egg
4 medium tomatoes, chopped
1 green bell pepper, chopped
½ cup chopped onion
½ cup chopped sweet pickles
9 slices bacon, cooked and crumbled
1 cup mayonnaise
¼ cup sweet pickle juice

Preheat oven to 400°. In a bowl, combine cornbread mix, milk and egg. Spoon into a greased, 8-inch square pan; bake 20 minutes. When cool, crumble into a bowl. In another bowl, combine tomatoes, bell pepper, onion, pickles and bacon; toss gently. In another bowl, mix mayonnaise and pickle juice; set aside. Using a large glass bowl so you can see the layers, make 6 layers using mixtures, starting with cornbread, then tomato mixture, and finishing with mayonnaise mixture. Cover and chill 2 hours before serving.

Local Favorite

2379 Highway 178 West
Holly Springs, MS 38635
662-252-2424
www.marshallsteakhouse.com
Find us on facebook

Welcome to Marshall Steakhouse, Holly Springs' premier eatery for juicy prime USDA Angus beef steaks. Marshall's steaks aren't just juicy; they're huge There's a reason the Mississippi Beef Council and the Mississippi Cattlemen's Association awarded the steakhouse the designation of the Best Steak in Mississippi. The Food Network even named Marshall Steakhouse the Best Steakhouse in Mississippi. Visitors are greeted at the door by the mouth-watering scent of grilling steaks. The rustic decor and handmade tables and chairs bring a warm and homey charm to the entire dining experience. In addition to steaks, the menu also features prime rib, seafood, grilled chicken, pork chops, and more. Marshall Steakhouse awaits your visit.

Wednesday: 4:00 pm to 10:00 pm
Thursday: 5:00 pm to 10:00 pm
Friday & Saturday: 11:00 am to 11:00 pm
Sunday: 11:00 am to 9:00 pm

Smoked Salmon Dip

3 ounces smoked salmon
½ cup mayonnaise
Juice of 1 lemon
2 leaves fresh basil
16 ounces cream cheese, softened
⅛ cup minced shallots
⅛ cup minced garlic
¼ cup diced red pepper
Fresh baked pita chips for serving

Add all ingredients except pita chips to a food processor. Process until smooth, then transfer to a serving bowl. Serve with pita chips.

Restaurant Recipe

Maryland Crabcakes

¼ cup mayonnaise

1 large egg, beaten

1 tablespoon stone-ground mustard

1 teaspoon Worcestershire sauce

4 dashes hot sauce

Juice of 1 lemon

1 teaspoon Old Bay seasoning

1 teaspoon each kosher salt and ground white pepper

1 pound lump crabmeat

½ pound crawfish tails

½ cup panko breadcrumbs

2 tablespoons finely chopped carrot

2 tablespoons finely chopped celery

2 tablespoons finely chopped onion

2 tablespoons canola oil

In a small mixing bowl, add mayonnaise, egg, mustard, Worcestershire, hot sauce, lemon juice, Old Bay, salt and pepper; whisk until combined. Add crab, crawfish, panko and vegetables; gently fold, taking care not to break crabmeat. Shape mixture into 4- to 6-ounce patties, then refrigerate at least 2 hours. Heat oil in a skillet over medium heat; add crabcakes, sautéing 3 to 5 minutes each side until browned.

Restaurant Recipe

Kahlua Cake

1 box butter cake mix

1 (5.9-ounce) box instant chocolate pudding mix

1 cup oil

½ cup sugar

¼ cup vodka

4 eggs

Glaze:

¼ cup Kahlua

¾ cup powdered sugar

Preheat oven to 350°. In a large mixing bowl, combine all cake ingredients and mix well; pour into a large greased Bundt pan and bake 50 minutes to 1 hour. Cool cake 10 minutes, then flip out onto a serving plate. Using a fork, poke holes in top of cake. Combine Glaze ingredients in a bowl and mix until smooth; drizzle over cake and enjoy.

Family Favorite

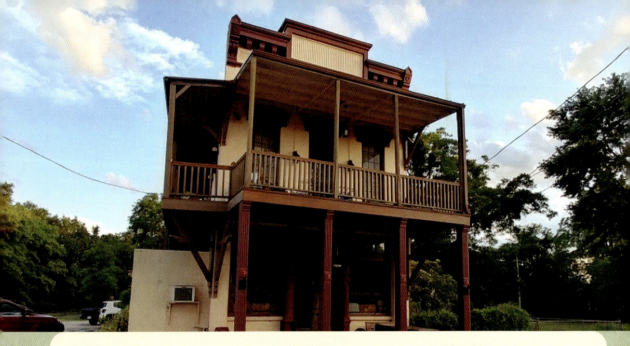

Phillips Grocery

541 East Van Dorn Avenue
Holly Springs, MS 38635
662-252-4671
Find us on facebook

Housed in a late nineteenth-century saloon, Phillips Grocery is home of the famous Phillips Burger. In its storied history, the building has served as a saloon, a grocery store, and ultimately a burger joint when Mr. and Mrs. W. L. Phillips purchased it in 1948. Ever since then, Phillips Grocery has served up amazing burgers with a side of nostalgia. Retro signs and memorabilia adorn the restaurant's walls, taking diners on a trip to the past as they enjoy their meals. There's a reason this Holly Springs tradition has stuck around for more than seventy years. Come get a taste of what you're missing.

Tuesday – Friday: 10:00 am to 4:00 pm
Saturday: 10:00 am to 5:30 pm

Cheese Bread

1¾ cups milk

3 cups shredded sharp Cheddar cheese, divided

3 tablespoons sugar

3 teaspoons salt

2 tablespoons butter plus extra to melt

1 (0.25-ounce) package active dry yeast

5½ cups flour, divided

Place milk in saucepan over medium heat. Cook 3 to 5 minutes until temperature is 212° (or a steady line of bubbles form around edge.) Add 2 cups cheese, sugar, salt and 2 tablespoons butter. Stir until cheese melts; set aside to cool. Sprinkle yeast in ¼ cup warm water to dissolve. Add yeast to cheese mixture and let stand 3 minutes. Add 5 cups flour and remaining cheese; mix well. Turn dough out onto surface sprinkled with remaining flour; knead until smooth and satin-like. Place dough into large bowl and brush with extra melted butter; cover with a cloth and let stand in warm place until doubled in size, about 1½ hours. Punch down and divide in half. Knead both halves; cover and let stand 10 minutes. Shape into loaves; place in greased loaf pans. Cover and let rest in a warm spot until doubled in size. Preheat oven to 300°. Bake 35 to 40 minutes or until brown on top. Remove from pans to cool.

Local Favorite

Banana Mallow Pie

1 (3.4-ounce) box instant vanilla pudding

1¾ cups milk

1½ cups miniature marshmallows

1 cup whipped cream

2 bananas, sliced into coins

1 (9-inch) graham cracker pie crust

Combine pudding with milk; refrigerate until chilled. Fold in marshmallows and whipped cream. Arrange banana slices in bottom of pie crust. Pour filling over top of bananas. Place in refrigerator several hours before serving or overnight. Enjoy.

Local Favorite

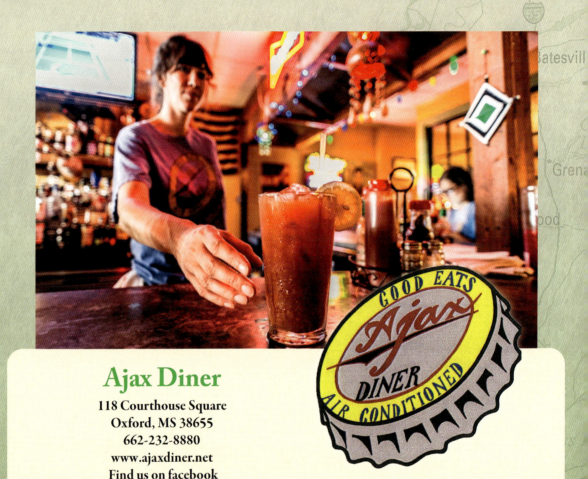

Ajax Diner

118 Courthouse Square
Oxford, MS 38655
662-232-8880
www.ajaxdiner.net
Find us on facebook

Located on the historic square, Ajax Diner has been serving Oxford for more than twenty years. Over the years, the accolades have piled up, from being named "Best Downhome Soul Food" by *Mississippi Magazine* three years in a row to "Best of the Best" by *the Oxford Eagle*. Ajax is even one of the Manning family's favorite restaurants. Guests will enjoy salads, sandwiches, po' boys, burgers, plate lunches, and more. Ajax also has a variety of dinner entrées, from steak to meatloaf to Southern fried chicken. Don't forget to try the homemade lemonade. Visit Ajax Diner for time-tested good eats.

Monday – Saturday: 11:30 am to 10:00 pm

Turnip Green Dip

15 slices bacon, diced small
1 large onion, diced small
2 tablespoons minced garlic
½ cup white wine
4 cups cooked turnip greens
2 pounds cream cheese
2 cups sour cream
2 cups grated Parmesan cheese plus more for topping
½ tablespoon crushed red pepper
1 teaspoon salt
3 to 4 cups diced fresh tomatoes

In a saucepan over medium heat, cook bacon until crisp; remove from pan. Increase heat to medium high and add onion and garlic; cook 3 to 4 minutes. Add wine and cook 2 minutes more. Stir in greens, cream cheese, sour cream, Parmesan and seasonings; cook, stirring often, until cream cheese is melted and smooth. Stir in tomatoes, then remove pan from heat and place in ice bath to cool. Serve Turnip Green Dip with a sprinkle of Parmesan and bacon over tops. Heat in oven before serving.

Restaurant Recipe

Tamale Pie

4 cups medium-diced yellow onion
3 tablespoons puréed garlic
1 stick butter
4 cups chopped roasted poblano peppers
4 cups whole-kernel corn
6 cups smoked pulled pork
5 tablespoons chili powder
3 tablespoons ground cumin
2 tablespoons kosher salt
1 tablespoon black pepper
2 teaspoons ground cayenne pepper
4 tomatoes, deseeded and chopped
8 cups cooked cheese grits, divided
Melted pepper Jack cheese for topping
Salsa verde for topping

Preheat oven to 375°. In a saucepan over medium heat, sauté onion and garlic purée in butter until onion is just tender. Add poblano, corn and pork; sauté 5 minutes more. Stir in seasonings and remove pan from heat; add tomatoes. In a buttered 9x13-inch baking dish, spread half of grits; allow to cool, then spread meat mixture over grits. Add remaining grits, spreading as evenly and smoothly as possible over top of meat mixture. Bake, uncovered, about 45 minutes. Cool at least 1 hour before cutting. Top with cheese and salsa before serving.

Restaurant Recipe

The Beacon Restaurant

1200 North Lamar Boulevard
Oxford, MS 38655
662-234-5041
Find us on facebook

The Beacon Restaurant has been serving the Oxford community since April 15, 1959. Opened by Flem and Charlene Mize, this unassuming eatery has lasted nearly six decades to become an Oxford staple. Today, The Beacon is run by their son, Tony Mize, and continues to serve up down-home breakfast and lunch with a Southern accent. The restaurant looks much the same as it always has because Tony wants to keep it that way. Some of the employees have even been around for more than thirty years, serving generations of families. With a menu that will remind of your mother's home cooking, The Beacon can't wait to serve you.

Monday – Friday: 6:00 am to 5:00 pm
Saturday: 6:00 am to 2:00 pm

Lemon Meringue Pie

4 eggs, room temperature
3 (14-ounce) cans Eagle Brand sweetened condensed milk
1 lemon, zested
1 cup freshly squeezed lemon juice
1 (9-inch) graham cracker pie crust
Pinch cream of tartar
½ cup sugar

Preheat oven to 400°. Between 2 bowls, carefully separate eggs without breaking yolks. To yolks, add condensed milk and mix with a wooden spoon. Add lemon zest and juice, then mix until blended. Pour filling into pie crust and bake 5 minutes; remove from oven. Beat egg whites with a hand mixer set to high speed until foamy; add cream of tartar and continue beating while slowly adding sugar. When stiff peaks form, top pie with meringue and return to oven for 3 minutes or until meringue has browned.

Restaurant Recipe

Bouré Restaurant

110 Courthouse Square
Oxford, MS 38655
662-234-1968
www.citygroceryonline.com/boure
Find us on facebook

Established in 2002, Bouré Restaurant is housed in the old Leslie's Drug Store and Downtown Grill building on the historic Oxford Square. The newly renovated space is home to the up-scale yet down-home fare of Bouré. Though decidedly Creole in its overall scope, the restaurant isn't easily labeled. A bustling, casual dining room and balcony, attentive service, and an outstanding menu elevate Bouré to something greater than just another college-town joint. Bouré is for everyone from a college date night to a special dinner with the family.

Monday – Thursday: 11:00 am to 10:00 pm
Friday & Saturday: 11:00 am to 10:30 pm
BAR:
Monday – Wednesday: 4:00 pm to midnight
Thursday & Friday: 4:00 pm to 1:00 am
Saturday: noon to 1:00 am

Mississippi Caviar

1 green bell pepper, diced small

1 red bell pepper, diced small

1 yellow bell pepper, diced small

16 green onions, chopped

2 tomatoes, diced small

2 avocados, diced small

2 cups cilantro, minced

1 (15-ounce) can black-eyed peas, drained

1 (16-ounce) bottle Italian dressing

Mix all ingredients in a stainless steel bowl. Place in sealable container, label and date.

Restaurant Recipe

Bouré Sauce

1 gallon chili sauce

2 gallons Blue Plate mayonnaise

1 quart yellow mustard

1 cup roasted garlic pepper

6 tablespoons onion powder

6 tablespoons garlic powder

6 tablespoons paprika

½ cup Tabasco sauce

2 cups lemon juice

8 cups red wine vinegar

1 cup chili powder

6 tablespoons cumin

Using a large stainless steel bowl, combined all ingredients with a hand wand until everything is completely incorporated. Store mixture in 22 quart jars. Label and date.

Restaurant Recipe

Grilled Peach Chutney

4 (3-pound) bags frozen peach slices

Olive oil

Salt and pepper to taste

12 cups white balsamic vinegar

12 cups sugar

22 yellow onions, julienned

8 cups chopped cooked bacon

½ cup fresh thyme, chopped

Toss peaches in a small amount of olive oil, salt and pepper; grill them. In a large stockpot, bring vinegar and sugar to a boil. Add onion and bacon. Dice peaches; add to stockpot along with thyme. Simmer over low heat, stirring often until reduced by half.

Restaurant Recipe

Bar-B-Q by Jim

203 Commerce Street
Tupelo, MS 38804
662-840-8800
Find us on facebook

Get a taste of Mississippi-style barbecue at Bar-B-Q by Jim, a smokehouse and grill that uses only the best cuts of meat and the freshest ingredients. At Bar-B-Q by Jim, they never get in a hurry because they know from experience that good barbecue takes time. For pulled pork, they use Boston butts, and for ribs, there's no better choice than St. Louis–style, with thick, well-marbled meat. For brisket, they remove the bone before cooking, which results in a brisket that cooks up better than a spare rib. With years of barbecue experience and time-tested recipes, Bar-B-Q by Jim will keep you coming back for more, time after time.

Monday – Wednesday: 10:30 am to 6:00 pm
Thursday – Saturday: 10:30 am to 7:30 pm

Baked Beans

1 (114-ounce) can pork and beans
8 ounces chopped onion
8 ounces chopped green bell pepper
1 cup Worcestershire sauce
8 ounces barbecue sauce
8 to 10 ounces dark (or light) brown sugar
Smoke sausage, sliced
1 pound prepared pulled pork

In a large baking dish, combine all ingredients except sausage and pulled pork, mixing well. Cover and refrigerate at least 2 days, allowing beans to marinate and flavors to develop. Preheat oven to 180°. Stir smoked sausage into beans, then bake 2½ hours. Remove from oven and stir in pulled pork. Bake 30 minutes more and enjoy.

Restaurant Recipe

Connie's Fried Chicken

821 South Gloster Street
Tupelo, MS 38801
662-842-7260
Find us on facebook

If it's Southern-style fried chicken you're craving, look no further than Connie's Fried Chicken. A Tupelo staple, Connie's has served its delicious chicken for decades. The chicken biscuits with gravy are a favorite of locals and visitors alike. Connie's chicken pairs well with an order of fried onion rings, but if you want something a bit more fresh, stop by the salad bar. While you're there, don't forget to try the famous blueberry donuts if you're lucky enough to snag one before they sell out. With just one bite, you'll understand why Connie's has been a Tupelo mainstay for years.

Monday – Friday: 6:00 am to 8:00 pm
Saturday: 6:00 am to 2:00 pm
Sunday: 7:00 am to 2:00 pm

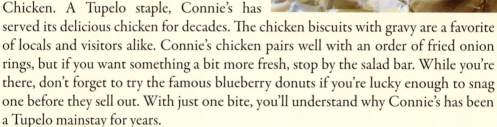

Barbecue Sauce

1 cup sugar
1 teaspoon cornstarch
½ teaspoon oregano
½ teaspoon thyme
2 teaspoons salt
¼ teaspoon cayenne pepper
1 teaspoon black pepper
¾ cup distilled vinegar
1½ cups molasses
1¼ cups ketchup
2 cups yellow mustard
¼ cup oil

In a medium saucepan, mix all dry ingredients; stir in vinegar slowly to form a paste. Stir in remaining ingredients; mix well. Bring mixture to a boil over medium heat. Reduce heat and simmer 20 minutes. Cool and store in refrigerator.

Local Favorite

Burger Pockets

½ pound ground beef
1 tablespoon chopped onion
½ teaspoon salt
⅛ teaspoon pepper
1 (12-ounce) tube refrigerated buttermilk biscuits
5 slices processed American cheese

Preheat oven to 400°. In a large skillet, cook beef, onion, salt and pepper over medium heat until meat is no longer pink; drain and cool. Place 2 biscuits overlapping on a floured surface; roll out into a 5-inch oval. On 1 half, place about ¼ cup meat mixture; top with 1 slice cheese, folded to fit. Fold dough over filling, making a half-circle shape; press edges with a fork to seal. Repeat with remaining biscuits, meat mixture and cheese. Place on a greased baking sheet. Prick tops with a fork to create steam vents. Bake 10 minutes or until golden brown.

Local Favorite

Crossroads Rib Shack

3061 Tupelo Commons
Tupelo, MS 38804
662-840-1700
Find us on facebook

If it isn't clear from the name, Crossroads Rib Shack takes its ribs seriously. With a dry rub made from a special blend of fresh spices, ribs from Crossroads undergo a treatment said to unlock their true character—"something too good to smother with sauce." Slow smoked to lock in that trademark flavor, the ribs are then served with some good old-fashioned sides and desserts. Factor in that one-of-a-kind Southern hospitality, and a meal enjoyed at Crossroads Rib Shack is a meal to remember.

Monday – Thursday: 11:00 am to 9:00 pm
Friday & Saturday: 11:00 am to 9:30 pm
Sunday: 11:00 am to 3:00 pm

Creamed Chip Beef

3 tablespoons margarine
3 tablespoons flour
2 cups half-and-half
1 (3-ounce) container dried beef, julienned
1 hard-boiled egg, chopped

In a skillet, melt margarine over medium heat. Stir in flour, a little at a time until smooth. Gradually add half-and-half. Add beef and cook until thickened. Fold in egg. Serve over toasted bread.

Local Favorite

Chicken Bog

Salt to taste
1 (2½- to 3½-pound) chicken
1 (10.75-ounce) can onion soup
1 cup uncooked rice

Salt chicken and place in a stockpot; cover with water. Bring to a boil and cook 30 minutes or until tender. Remove chicken and debone, reserving stock. Preheat oven to 350°. Place chicken, 1½ cups stock, onion soup and rice in a 9x13-inch baking dish. Bake 1 hour.

Local Favorite

NEON PIG

1203 North Gloster Street
Tupelo, MS 38804
662-269-2533
www.eatneonpig.com
Find us on facebook

Neon Pig is an old-school butcher shop, a fresh never-frozen seafood shop, a food bar, and home to one of the best craft beer selections in Mississippi. The team at Neon Pig strives to bring old-fashioned goodness back into the food industry by specializing in house-cured meats. Owners Trish McCluney, Mitch McCamey, and Seth Copeland stress that Neon Pig is not a chain restaurant. By purchasing from local farmers and businesses, they give back to the community, by stimulating the local economy and creating a sense of local pride. Save Tupelo; buy local

Monday – Saturday: 11:00 am to 9:00 pm
Sunday: 11:00 am to 4:00 pm

Pimento Cheese

20 pounds Cheddar cheese, shredded
4 quarts mayonnaise
6 (28-ounce) cans pimentos
2 quarts bacon bits
¾ cup black pepper
¾ cup garlic powder
¾ cup onion powder
4 cups sugar
1 cup melted bacon fat

Mix all ingredients together until well combined. Serve.

Restaurant Recipe

Potato Salad

15 pounds red potatoes, peeled and cubed
1 bunch green onions, chopped
2 red onions, chopped
1 quart bacon bits
12 cups mayonnaise
4 cups Creole mustard
1 (16-ounce) jar mayhew chow
2 cups dry milk
1½ tablespoons cayenne pepper
2 tablespoons celery salt

In a large stockpot over medium heat, cook potatoes until fork tender. Drain potatoes. In a large mixing bowl, mix all ingredients together until well combined.

Restaurant Recipe

Romie's Grocery

804 West Jackson Street
Tupelo, MS 38804
662-842-8986
www.romies.net
Find us on facebook

On May 16, 2005, Romie's Grocery opened its doors, serving lunch six days a week. Folks really seemed to love their daily meat-and-three plate lunches with such a variety of meats and vegetables to choose from. Guests to Romie's Grocery have included people like Hailey Barbour, Phil Bryant, Roger Wicker, Travis Childers, Miranda Lambert, Marty Stewart, Daryl Waltrip, and a host of other local celebs and regulars. Providing every guest with the best Southern cuisine and Southern hospitality is and always will be the mission at Romie's Grocery. Now serving lunch seven days a week, Romie's Grocery is the place to be for lunch in Tupelo.

Monday – Saturday: 11:00 am to 5:00 pm
Sunday: 11:00 am to 2:00 pm

Brandied Fruit

1 (20-ounce) can peach slices, drained

1 (20-ounce) can pineapple chunks, drained

1 (20-punce) can apricot halves, drained

1 (20-ounce) can pear halves, drained

1 (18-ounce) jar apple rings, drained

½ stick butter

½ cup sugar

2 tablespoons flour

1 cup sherry

Place fruit in a 9x13-inch casserole dish. Using a double boiler over medium heat, cook butter, sugar, flour and sherry until thick; pour over fruit. Cover casserole and refrigerate overnight. Bake at 350° for 45 minutes. Serve warm.

Local Favorite

Cheese Marbles

2 cups grated Cheddar cheese

½ cup butter, softened

1 cup flour

¼ teaspoon salt

2 teaspoons dry mustard

Preheat oven to 350°. In a bowl, blend cheese and butter until smooth and creamy. In a bowl, sift together flour, salt and mustard; add to cheese mixture, mixing thoroughly. Form into marble-size balls and place on a greased cookie sheet. Bake 15 minutes and enjoy.

Local Favorite

Sweet Tea & Biscuits Café
The Epitome of Southern Hospitality

2025 McCullough Boulevard
Tupelo, MS 38801
662-322-7322
www.sweetteaandb.com
Find us on facebook

Sweet Tea & Biscuits is a family-operated café and catering business offering homemade Southern favorites. Founded in 2011 by Beverly Blaylock, all dishes are homemade with love by Beverly and her sister, Joan Lansdell. The sisters use recipes passed down by their mother to create a variety of homemade soups, sandwiches, snacks, and desserts—all made from scratch. If all that wasn't enough, the café also features a freezer full of marvelous casseroles and desserts to take home. Sweet Tea & Biscuits also prepares luscious appetizers, desserts, and full-course meals for all your catering needs. Stop by to fill your belly and be part of the family

Tuesday – Saturday: 11:00 am to 2:00 pm

Strawberry Pretzel Salad

2 cups crushed pretzels
¾ cup (1½ sticks) melted butter
1 cup plus 3 tablespoons sugar, divided
1 (8-ounce) package cream cheese, softened
1 (8-ounce) container Cool Whip
2 (3-ounce) boxes strawberry Jell-O
2 (16-ounce) packages frozen sliced strawberries

Preheat oven to 400°. In a bowl, stir together pretzels, butter and 3 tablespoons sugar. Press into the bottom of a 9x13-inch baking dish and bake 8 to 10 minutes; set aside to cool completely. In a large mixing bowl, cream together cream cheese and remaining sugar. Fold in Cool Whip and spread mixture over cooled pretzel crust; refrigerate until set. Following package directions, prepare Jell-O; stir in frozen strawberries and refrigerate until slightly set. Spread strawberry mixture over cream cheese layer. Refrigerate overnight or until strawberry layer is completely set.

Restaurant Recipe

Homemade Biscuits

¼ cup Crisco shortening
2 cups White Lily self-rising flour
¾ cup buttermilk
2 tablespoons melted butter

Preheat oven to 475°. In a large bowl, cut shortening into flour using a pastry blender or 2 knives until crumbs are pea-sized. Add buttermilk, stirring with a fork until flour is moistened. Turn dough onto a lightly floured surface and knead gently 5 to 6 times until a smooth dough forms. Roll into 7-inch-wide circle that is ¾- to 1-inch thick. Using a floured 2-inch biscuit cutter, cut out 7 to 8 biscuits. Arrange on a baking sheet about 1 inch apart; for softer biscuits, arrange so edges almost touch. Bake 8 to 10 minutes or until golden brown. Remove from oven and brush tops with butter.

Restaurant Recipe

PINES

Carthage
 Singleton Steak & Fish House 84

Columbus
 Café Unique Home Cooking 86
 Farmstead Restaurant 88
 Zachary's 90

Enterprise
 Coffee Pot Café 92

Eupora
 Mama Guinn's Café 94

Forest
 The Food Hut 96
 Fye Grubz 98

French Camp
 Council House Restaurant 100

Louisville
 Market Café 102

Mantee
 Pop's Family Diner 104

Meridian
 The Checker Board 106
 Harvest Grill 108
 Weidmann's Restaurant 110

Newton
 T-Bones, Too 112

Sebastopol
 Lee's Steakhouse 114

Starkville
 The Little Dooey 116

Union
 T-Bones Steakhouse 118

Walnut Grove
 Urban Country Kitchen 120

Author Anita's grandsons, Nic and Ryan

Singleton Steak & Fish House

107 North Pearl Street
Carthage, MS 39051
601-267-5007
Find us on facebook

Located on the square in the historic Chipley's Clothing Store building, Singleton Steak & Fish House is ready to serve you. According to the restaurant's motto, Singleton Steak & Fish House is a place "where all are welcome and everyone has a seat at the table." The newly remodeled restaurant offers a lunch buffet Monday through Friday; a catfish, chicken nugget, fried shrimp buffet Thursday and Friday nights; a seafood buffet Saturday nights; and a Sunday lunch buffet. Recent additions include a breakfast buffet Saturday mornings with a lunch buffet starting later that day. Needless to say, there's no shortage of tasty food. Come out for great food and friendly service.

Monday – Wednesday:
10:30 am to 3:00 pm
Thursday & Friday: 10:30 am to 9:00 pm
Saturday: 11:00 am to 9:30 pm
Sunday: 11:00 am to 3:30 pm

Coconut Custard Pie

1 stick butter, softened

1½ cups sugar

2 eggs

2 tablespoons all-purpose flour

1 cup milk

1 cup plus 1 tablespoon flaked coconut, divided

1 teaspoon vanilla extract

1 (9-inch) pie crust, unbaked

Preheat oven to 350°. In a large bowl, beat together butter, sugar and eggs with an electric hand mixer on low speed. Mix in flour, then ½ cup milk at a time until smooth. Mix in 1 cup coconut and vanilla. Pour mixture into pie crust and sprinkle top with remaining coconut. Bake 40 to 50 minutes or until set.

Restaurant Recipe

Old-Time Buttermilk Pie

½ cup margarine, softened

2 cups sugar

3 tablespoons all-purpose flour

¼ teaspoon salt

3 eggs

1 cup buttermilk

1 teaspoon vanilla extract

1 (9-inch) deep-dish pie crust, unbaked

Preheat oven to 400°. In a large bowl, beat together margarine and sugar with an electric hand mixer. Beat in flour and salt, then eggs. Mix in buttermilk and vanilla. Pour mixture into pie crust. Bake 15 minutes, then reduce oven temperature to 325° and bake 45 minutes or until filling is set.

Restaurant Recipe

Café Unique
HOMECOOKING

94 Airline Road
Columbus, MS 39702
662-327-4863
Find us on facebook

Café Unique Home Cooking first opened its doors in 2013 serving up a variety of soul food with a good, down-home Southern taste. Favorites such as smothered pork chops, fried chicken, catfish, and chitterlings can be found on the menu. Catering services are offered for small private parties, office luncheons, dinners, or group outings. You may choose to use their facilities during non-business hours. No job is too small or too large.

Monday – Thursday: 11:00 am to 2:00 pm
Friday: 11:00 am to 2:30 pm
1st and 3rd Sunday: 11:30 am to 2:30 pm

Butter Rolls

2 cups self-rising flour, plus more for rolling
½ cup shortening
¾ cup whole milk
1 stick butter, softened
¼ cup plus 2 tablespoons packed light brown sugar
¼ teaspoon ground nutmeg,
1 teaspoon ground cinnamon
1 (14-ounce) can sweetened condensed milk
2 cups half and half
¾ cup powdered sugar
2 tablespoons butter
Pinch of salt
1 teaspoon vanilla

Preheat oven to 350°. In a large mixing bowl, sift flour and cut in shortening with a fork or pastry blender, until resembles coarse crumbs. Pour whole milk into flour mixture and stir until dough is soft, moist and pulls away from the side of bowl. Turn dough out onto a lightly floured surface and toss with flour until no longer sticky. Roll dough into a rectangle ½-inch thick. Spread dough evenly with butter. Stir together brown sugar, nutmeg and cinnamon, sprinkle evenly over butter. Carefully roll dough, jelly-roll fashion. Slice roll into 12 even slices and place in a greased 9x13-inch casserole dish 3 across and 4 down. Spread a light coat of butter over rolls. Bake until rolls begin to brown on top. While rolls bake, in a saucepan over medium high heat, place condensed milk, half and half, powdered sugar butter and salt. Stir gently until mixture just begins to bubble and sugar is completely dissolved. Remove from heat and stir in vanilla. Pour over rolls, they will be swimming in sauce. Place rolls back in oven and bake 40 minutes until rolls are puffed and golden brown, and the sauce is bubbling and beginning to caramelize. Let cool for several minutes. Serve each roll with a spoonful of sauce.

Restaurant Recipe

Corn Salad

2 (15-ounce) cans whole kernel corn, drained
1 cup salad dressing, or mayonnaise
1 cup chopped bell pepper
1 cup diced tomatoes
½ cup chopped green onions
Cayenne pepper to taste

Mix all ingredients in a resealable container. Chill completely before serving.

Restaurant Recipe

Farmstead Restaurant

142 South McCrary Road
Columbus, MS 39702
662-240-8860
www.farmstead-columbus.com
Find us on facebook

Farmstead Restaurant is a family-style restaurant featuring anything from fried chicken to turnip greens and rotating menu for lunch specials. If you prefer something from the grill they have a great burgers. And don't forget the fresh salads. Affordable catering services are provided for any type of service including wedding receptions, anniversaries, birthday parties, banquets, conventions, or school functions. For an authentic Southern meal at an affordable price make your next stop Farmstead Restaurant.

Sunday – Friday:
11:00 am to 2:00 pm

Mississippi BACK ROAD RESTAURANT Recipes

Sweet Potato Casserole

20 pounds sweet potatoes, roasted
2 pounds margarine, melted
3 cups brown sugar
1 tablespoon kosher salt
2 tablespoons cinnamon
2 (12-ounce) cans evaporated milk

Recipe is for 100 servings. Preheat oven to 350°. Peel potatoes and mash in large mixer. Add margarine, sugar, salt, cinnamon and milk. Taste for sweetness and texture. Pour into pans and bake 20 to 30 minutes or until hot (160°) in middle. Add topping.

Topping:

2 cups brown sugar
3 cups all-purpose flour
1 pound margarine, melted

In a large bowl combine sugar and flour. Add margarine slowly, mixing by hand, until mixture starts to come together when squeezed, but still crumbly. Sprinkle over casserole.

Restaurant Recipe

Lemon Parade

2 sticks butter, melted
¾ cup flour
¾ cup finely chopped pecans
1 (8-ounce) package cream cheese, softened
1 cup sugar
1 (24-ounce) container Cool Whip, divided
6 egg yolks
2 (14-ounce) cans sweetened condensed milk
½ cup fresh-squeezed lemon juice

Preheat oven to 350°. In a bowl mix together butter, flour and pecans. Press into bottom of 9x13-inch baking dish. Bake 25 minutes. Remove from oven; cool completely. In another bowl, mix cream cheese, sugar and half of Cool Whip. Spread over cooled crust. Beat egg yolks; add condensed milk and mix well. Add lemon juice; beating well. Spread over second layer. Refrigerate until ready to serve. Spread remaining Cool Whip over top and serve.

Restaurant Recipe

Pines

205 North 5th Street
Columbus, MS 39701
662-240-0101
www.zacharyscolumbus.com
Find us on facebook

Established in 2001, Zachary's restaurant is a Columbus mainstay serving up American food classics in a wonderful atmosphere. From burgers to wraps and so much more, Zachary's has it all. As a community staple, the restaurant doesn't just stop at serving customers. Zachary's restaurant is also a fundraising titan. Between 2017 and 2020, the restaurant raised over $110,000 for multiple local fundraisers and earned the National Restaurant Association Neighbor Award three years straight. In April 2019, the restaurant suffered a fire but was able to rebuild and keep its employees thanks to a community fundraiser. Now reopened, Zachary's continues to go above and beyond, serving delicious food and unconditional charity.

Monday – Thursday: 11:00 am to 9:00 pm
Friday & Saturday: 11:00 am to 10:00 pm

Roasted Red Pepper Hummus

1 (15.4-ounce) can garbanzo beans, drained
1 (16-ounce) can roasted red peppers, drained
4 ounces tahini paste
Juice of 1 lemon
1 tablespoon blackened seasoning
2 tablespoons garlic powder
2 teaspoons paprika
Salt to taste
½ cup olive oil

In a large bowl, mix all ingredients, except olive oil, with an immersion blender until chunky consistency. Transfer to blender in small batches and purée adding olive oil slowly until smooth.

Restaurant Recipe

Loaded Potato Soup

10 baked potatoes, peeled and diced
Bacon, fried crisp and chopped
1 (14.5- ounce) can chicken broth
1 (10.75- ounce) can cream of mushroom soup
2 cups shredded Cheddar cheese
Salt and pepper to taste
Grated red onion for garnish

In a large stockpot over medium-high heat, boil potatoes and bacon in chicken broth for 10 minutes stirring often. Lower heat to medium; add 2 cups water, mushroom soup and cheese. Continue to cook, stirring constantly, until heated through. Add salt and pepper; stir. Add more water if too thick and more cheese if too thin. Garnish with red onion.

Restaurant Recipe

Coffee Pot Café

120 West Bridge Street
Enterprise, MS 39330
601-659-0500
Find us on facebook

Welcome to Coffee Pot Café. Step back in time and enjoy the atmosphere and music as well as food prepared with love just for you. As you browse around, notice the antique food scales and cheese cutter from the previous owner's grandparents' (Mr. and Mrs. W.R. Hatton) country store of the 1930s and '40s era. The daily specials may change due to experimenting with new menu items or bringing something greater to the table, but there will always be homemade desserts and main dishes like gumbo, étouffée, red beans and rice, chicken salad, the Driftwood (a hamburger served on a po' boy bun), and grilled cheeses made with old-fashioned hoop cheese.

LUNCH:
Wednesday – Saturday: 11:00 am to 2:00 pm
DINNER:
Friday & Saturday: 5:00 pm to 9:00 pm

Shrimp & Grits

5 slices bacon
¼ cup flour
1 green bell pepper, chopped
1 red bell pepper, chopped
½ onion, chopped
2 (6-ounce) tomatoes, diced
1 cup chicken (or shrimp) stock
1 tablespoon minced garlic
1 teaspoon Cajun seasoning
1 pound shrimp, peeled and deveined
Shredded Cheddar cheese, butter, salt and pepper to taste
Prepared grits for serving

In a large sauté pan, cook bacon until crisp; remove from pan. Add flour to bacon grease and whisk over medium heat 2 minutes. Add bell peppers and onion; cook 5 minutes. Stir in tomatoes and stock. Stir in garlic and seasoning. Bring to a simmer and add shrimp; set heat to low and continue simmering 15 minutes. Add cheese, butter, salt and pepper to grits. Top grits with shrimp mixture and crumbled bacon.

Restaurant Recipe

Crab Cakes

2 eggs
½ cup mayonnaise
1 tablespoon Creole mustard
1 teaspoon hot sauce
1 teaspoon chopped fresh parsley
1 (16-ounce) can lump crabmeat
¼ cup breadcrumbs plus more for coating
Olive oil for cooking

In a large bowl, whisk together eggs, mayonnaise, mustard, hot sauce and parsley until combined. Gently fold in crabmeat and ¼ cup breadcrumbs. Refrigerate 30 minutes. Once mixture has thickened, form into 4-ounce patties and coat with additional breadcrumbs. In a skillet over low heat, fry patties in olive oil until golden brown on both sides.

Restaurant Recipe

Mama Guinn's Café

**1401 Veterans Memorial Boulevard
Eupora, MS 39744
662-744-7068
Find us on facebook**

Welcome to Mama Guinn's Café, a diner-style restaurant serving up breakfast and lunch. As Eupora's only charbroil restaurant in town, Mama Guinn's serves up delicious fare that is prepared fresh when ordered. There are a wide variety of choices on the breakfast menu, from an abundance of stuffed biscuits to classic breakfast plates. For lunch, you can tuck in to a plate of their famous wings or choose from various platters, such as steaks, pork chops, and hamburgers. Ask about the daily special when you visit. Mama Guinn's Café awaits your visit.

Monday – Friday: 5:30 am to 2:00 pm
Saturday: 6:00 am to 1:00 pm

Fried Dill Pickles

Egg Wash:
2 cups milk
2 eggs
Pinch lemon pepper
Pinch dried dill weed
Pickle juice to taste

In a bowl, whisk together all ingredients.

Breading:
2½ cups cornmeal
1½ cups all-purpose flour
½ cup lemon pepper
½ cup dried dill weed
4 teaspoons paprika
2 teaspoons garlic salt
Ground Cayenne pepper to taste

In a medium bowl, whisk together all ingredients until combined.

Pickles:
Dill pickle slices
Ranch dressing for serving

Pat pickles dry, then dip in egg wash mixture. Dredge in breading mixture and arranged on a parchment-lined baking sheet; chill 30 minutes. Preheat deep fryer to 375°. Fry pickles 3½ minutes or until golden brown. Drain on paper towels, then serve with ranch while warm.

Restaurant Recipe

Fruit Top Biscuits

2½ pounds self-rising flour
1 pound shortening
2¾ cups buttermilk
Fruit pie filling of choice
Margarine, room temperature in a squeeze bottle
Store-bought cream cheese frosting in a piping bag

In a large stainless steel mixing bowl, combine flour and shortening, blending with hands until shortening is pea-sized. Add buttermilk and continue mixing by hand until mixture reaches a cottage cheese–like texture; refrigerate 20 minutes to firm up dough. On a clean, floured surface, turn mixture out of bowl and gently knead 3 to 4 times. Flour surface again and roll out dough to a ½-inch-thick circle. Using a floured 3-inch biscuit cutter, cut out biscuits as close together as possible; arrange cutouts on a lightly greased baking sheet. Using the back of a spoon, make a well in the top of each biscuit and spoon fruit filling into each. Bake at 450° for 10 minutes or until golden brown, rotating pan halfway through. Remove biscuits from oven; pipe margarine around the edge of each biscuit and set aside 5 minutes. Pipe frosting 4 lines left to right, then 4 lines top to bottom.

Restaurant Recipe

The Food Hut

154 East Third Street
Forest, MS 39074
601-469-4229
Find us on facebook

The Food Hut is your one-stop shop for all your favorite lunch and dinner foods. Enjoy hamburgers, chili cheese tots and fries, nachos, fish plates, ribs plates, fried or grilled chicken plates, BLTs, hamburger steak plates, Philly steak and cheese po' boys, shrimp po' boys, fish sandwiches, hot wings, and fried or grilled chicken salads. No matter what you're craving, The Food Hut has your needs covered.

Monday & Tuesday: 10:00 am to 7:00 pm
Thursday – Saturday: 10:00 am to 8:00 pm

Homemade Chicken Spaghetti

Raw chicken breasts (or cuts of choice)
1 to 2 (10-ounce) cans Rotel tomatoes
1 (10.5-ounce) can cream of chicken soup
2 cups shredded Cheddar cheese, divided
Prepared spaghetti

To a stockpot, add chicken and cover with water; bring to a boil. Simmer 10 to 15 minutes or until tender; reserving broth, remove chicken from pot. Cool and shred chicken. To a 9x13-inch baking dish, add Rotel, soup, 1 cup Cheddar, shredded chicken, spaghetti and some reserved chicken broth; mix well, then top with remaining Cheddar. Bake at 350° for 30 to 40 minutes or until cheese is melted and bubbly.

Family Favorite

Homemade Spaghetti

2 pounds ground beef
2 (15-ounce) cans tomato sauce, divided
1 yellow onion, chopped
1 green bell pepper, chopped
3 to 4 celery stalks, chopped
1 (6-ounce) can tomato paste
Garlic salt to taste
Prepared spaghetti for serving

In a stockpot over medium heat, brown meat; drain fat, then stir in 1 can tomato sauce. In another pot, add onion, bell pepper, celery, tomato paste and remaining can tomato sauce; bring to a simmer and cook until vegetables are tender. Combine in stockpot with meat mixture and season with garlic salt to taste. Serve over prepared spaghetti.

Family Favorite

Fye Grubz

9907 Old Hillsboro Road
Forest, MS 39074
601-697-7980
Find us on facebook

Are you looking for a unique eating experience in small-town Mississippi? Look no further than Fye Grubz. Located in the Harperville community of Forest, this walk-up order-out restaurant will surprise you. Yes, you can get the usual burger and fries, but Fye Grubz offers so much more. Their chicken and shrimp salad is loaded with delicious chopped chicken and a huge pile of shrimp. Maybe you are in the mood for chicken or shrimp tacos or a Philly cheese steak po' boy, delicious nachos with meat and cheese sauce, fried chicken or hot chicken wings. Whatever your craving, stop by Fye Grubz for some outstanding food that is guaranteed to hit the spot.

Call for hours.

Chicken-Bacon-Ranch Baked Potato

1 large baking potato
1 (6-ounce) chicken breast
Fye Grubz seasoning
Cheddar cheese sauce
Shredded Cheddar cheese
Bacon bits
Quesadilla cheese
Ranch dressing
Chopped onions

Bake potato in 425° oven 1½ hours or until fork tender in middle. Season chicken with seasoning and dice as it stir-fries. Slice potato lengthwise and squeeze open. Add cheese sauce, shredded cheese, bacon bits diced chicken, quesadilla cheese, ranch dressing and chopped onion.

Restaurant Recipe

Philly Cheese Sandwich

1 (5-ounce) thin-sliced sirloin beef
Fye Grubz seasoning
⅓ bell pepper, thinly sliced
¼ small onion, thinly sliced
⅓ cup shredded Swiss cheese
1 Philly bun

Place sirloin beef on grill, add seasoning and chop as it cooks. Add bell pepper and onions; cook until tender and beef is fully cooked and brown. Add cheese and scoop onto bun.

Restaurant Recipe

Council House Restaurant

55 Lefleur Circle
French Camp, MS 39745
601-547-9860
www.frenchcamphistoricvillage.com
Find us on facebook

The Council House was originally the meeting place for Greenwood LeFlore—the last chief of the Choctaw Indian Nation east of the Mississippi—and his chiefs during tribal negotiations. The restaurant features a rustic French Country décor serving delicious food with the warmth of Southern hospitality. If you are in the mood to dine outside, a large deck with fireplace is available to enjoy the beautiful outdoors. Don't forget to stop at the gift shop on your way out and pick up handmade Mississippi pottery, apparel, jellies, and jams.

Monday – Thursday: 10:30 am to 8:00 pm
Friday – Saturday: 10:30 am to 9:00 pm

Cream Cabbage Soup

2 (14.5-ounce) cans chicken broth
2 celery stalks, chopped
1 medium head cabbage, shredded
1 medium onion, chopped
1 carrot, chopped
¼ cup butter
3 tablespoons all-purpose flour
1 teaspoon salt
¼ teaspoon pepper
1 cup whipping cream
2 cups milk
2 cups cubed, fully cooked ham
½ teaspoon dried thyme
½ teaspoon dried parsley

In a large stockpot, combine broth, celery, cabbage, onion and carrot; bring to a boil. Reduce heat, cover pot; simmer 15 to 20 minutes or until vegetables are tender. Meanwhile in a saucepan over medium heat, melt butter. Stir in flour, salt and pepper to form a paste. Combine cream and milk; gradually add to flour mixture, stirring constantly until thick. Slowly stir milk mixture into vegetable mixture. Add ham, thyme and parsley; heat through.

Restaurant Recipe

French Camp Bread

2 to 2½ cups flour, divided
2 tablespoons sugar
½ teaspoon salt
1 (0.75 ounce) package active dry yeast
½ cup milk
¼ cup water
2 tablespoons margarine

Preheat oven to 350°. In a mixing bowl, mix ¾ cup flour, sugar, salt and undissolved yeast; set aside. In a saucepan over medium heat, heat milk, water and margarine to lukewarm. Slowly add milk mixture to dry mixture; beat 2 minutes. Add ¼ cup flour; beat another 2 minutes. Stir in enough flour to make a soft dough. Place dough onto a floured board; knead 2 to 3 minutes. Put dough into a loaf pan; let rise 1 hour. Bake 35 to 40 minutes.

Restaurant Recipe

MARKET CAFÉ

16533 West Main
Louisville, MS 39339
662-779-1500
www.eatatmarketcafe.com
Find us on facebook

Market Café is located on the corner of Main Street and Court Street in a renovated 1890s building across from the courthouse. They serve hot plate lunches, chalkboard specials, sandwiches, salads, and so much more. Weekends at the Market are spent serving lots of steaks and seafood. If you are in need of a wedding or special event catering they are one of Mississippi's best. Stop by and see the beautifully decorated building and don't forget to come hungry.

LUNCH:
Tuesday – Friday: 11:00 am to 2:00 pm
DINNER:
Friday – Saturday: 5:00 pm to 8:30 pm

Mexican Street Tacos

2 tablespoons reduced-sodium soy sauce
2 tablespoons fresh lime juice
2 tablespoons canola oil, divided
3 garlic cloves, minced
2 teaspoons chili powder
1 teaspoon ground cumin
1 teaspoon dried oregano
1½ pounds skirt steak, cut into ½-inch pieces
12 mini flour tortillas, warmed
¾ cup diced red onion
½ cup chopped fresh cilantro leaves
1 lime, cut into wedges

In a medium bowl, combine soy sauce, lime juice, 1 tablespoon canola oil, garlic, chili powder, cumin and oregano. Using a gallon-size zip-close bag or large bowl, combine soy sauce mixture and steak; marinate at least 1 hour or up to 4 hours, turning occasionally. Heat remaining canola oil in a large skillet over medium-high heat. Add steak and marinade; cook 5 to 6 minutes, stirring often, until steak is cooked and marinade has reduced, or until desired doneness. Serve steak in tortillas, topped with onion, cilantro and a squeeze of lime.

Restaurant Recipe

Crab Cakes

1 large egg, beaten
¼ cup mayonnaise
2 teaspoons Dijon mustard
2 teaspoons Worcestershire sauce
1 teaspoon Old Bay seasoning
1 tablespoon chopped fresh parsley
1 teaspoon fresh lemon juice, plus more for serving
⅛ teaspoon salt
1 pound fresh lump crabmeat
⅔ cup saltine cracker crumbs
2 tablespoons melted butter

In a medium bowl, whisk together egg, mayonnaise, mustard, Worcestershire, Old Bay, parsley, lemon juice and salt. Place crabmeat on top followed by cracker crumbs. Using a rubber spatula, very gently fold mixture together being careful to avoid breaking up crabmeat. Cover tightly and refrigerate at least 30 minutes (use within 24 hours). Preheat oven to 450°. Generously spray a rimmed baking sheet with nonstick cooking spray, or line with a silicone baking mat. Using a ½ cup scoop or measuring cup, portion crab mixture into 6 mounds—do not flatten. Use your hands, making sure each mound is compact and there aren't any lumps sticking out. For extra flavor, brush each mound with butter. Bake 12 to 14 minutes or until lightly browned. Drizzle with additional lemon juice and serve warm. May be kept in refrigerator covered up to 5 days or frozen up to 3 months.

Restaurant Recipe

Pop's Family Diner

24 Main Street
Mantee, MS 39751
662-631-5056
Find us on facebook

Pop's Family Diner is a warm and welcoming family restaurant serving a variety of delicious dishes, from fish and steaks to shrimp and burgers to so much more. Be sure to try the country-fried steak. The restaurant also offers a variety of homemade decadent desserts made fresh each week by Lee's Country Sweet Treats. From cakes to pies to cupcakes, you don't want to miss out. Come out to Pop's Family Diner for a taste of old-fashioned home cooking.

Friday & Saturday: 4:00 pm to 9:00 pm

Shrimp Boil Hobo Packs

2 ears fresh corn, husked

1 pound baby potatoes

1 pound shrimp, peeled and de-veined

½ pound andouille sausage, sliced

½ cup plus 3 tablespoons melted butter, divided

3 tablespoons Old Bay seasoning

1 tablespoon minced garlic

1 lemon, ½ juiced and ½ cut into wedges, for serving

Salt and pepper to taste

Chopped fresh parsley, for topping

Preheat oven to 400°. Chop corn into thirds, then chop each third in half lengthwise. Chop potatoes into 2-inch pieces. Boil corn and potatoes 10 minutes. Drain and set aside. In a large bowl, combine shrimp, sausage, corn, and potatoes. Stir together 3 tablespoons butter, Old Bay, garlic, lemon juice, salt and pepper; pour over shrimp mixture. Stir to coat. Divide between 4 (12x12-inch) sheets of aluminum foil. Fold edges of foil up around the food to create a closed packet. Bake 15 to 20 minutes until corn is tender and shrimp are pink and fully cooked. While packets are cooking, place remaining butter in a saucepan over medium-high heat, stirring gently 3 to 4 minutes until color changes from pale yellow to a golden amber (be careful not to burn it). Serve shrimp boil packs topped with chopped parsley, lemon wedges for squeezing, and browned butter for drizzling over the top or dipping. Yields 4 servings.

Restaurant Recipe

House-Made Ranch

8 cups Kraft mayonnaise

4 cups buttermilk

2 teaspoons black pepper

1 teaspoon cayenne pepper

1 teaspoon paprika

½ teaspoon garlic powder

2 (1.74- ounce) packages buttermilk ranch powder

Mix all ingredients together and chill overnight. Yields 1 gallon.

Restaurant Recipe

Pines   105

The Checker Board

2223 South Frontage Road
Meridian, MS 39301
601-481-1039
Find us on facebook

Welcome to The Checker Board, a Southern kitchen serving breakfast and lunch to the Meridian community seven days a week. If you're in search of old-fashioned comfort food, The Checker Board is the place to be. Enjoy buffet-style fried catfish, fried chicken, pork chops, meatloaf, fried green tomatoes, fried okra, dressing, butter beans, and so much more. You're sure to leave satisfied but dreaming about your next trip back. The team at The Checker Board can't wait to welcome you in.

7 Days a Week:
6:00 am to 2:30 pm

Fried Apple Rings

2 small apples
2 tablespoons margarine
2 tablespoons sugar
1 tablespoon lemon juice

Core apples and cut each into 4 circular slices. In a frying pan over medium heat, melt margarine; add sugar and lemon juice. Place apple rings in pan; slowly cook 10 to 15 minutes, adjusting heat accordingly. Turn as needed until apple slices are tender.

Local Favorite

Ham, Cheese & Rice

1 medium onion, thinly sliced
1 tablespoon oil
¾ cup rice
1½ cups cubed cooked ham
¼ teaspoon salt
½ cup milk
⅔ cup cubed cheese

In a saucepan over medium heat, cook onion in oil until lightly browned. Add 1¾ cups water and heat to boiling. Stir in rice, ham and salt. Cover, reduce heat to low and cook 25 minutes or until rice is tender. Gently stir in milk and cheese. Heat until cheese is melted.

Local Favorite

GREAT FOOD AND GATHERINGS
HARVEST GRILL
MERIDIAN, MISSISSIPPI

618 22nd Avenue
Meridian, MS 39301
601-282-5069
www.harvestgrillms.com
Find us on facebook

Located in historic downtown Meridian, Harvest Grill is a not just a restaurant with an inventive menu. It's also a place to meet friends and family to make memories over unforgettable "cross-country" cuisine. Inspired by the travels of chef Marshall Gilmore and his wife, Mary, the fare is anything but ordinary. The menu features fresh seafood, original sandwiches, burgers, soups, and so much more. Harvest Grill sources seasonal produce from Mississippi-based suppliers, so guests get the freshest taste every time. The restaurant also boasts a bar and an outdoor covered patio for when the weather is just right. At Harvest Grill, you're sure to feel right at home.

LUNCH:
Monday – Friday: 11:00 am to 2:00 pm
DINNER:
Tuesday – Thursday: 5:00 pm to 9:00 pm
Friday & Saturday: 5:00 pm to 10:00 pm

Grand Marnier Citrus Beignet

4 cups all-purpose flour

8 egg yolks

½ cup sugar

½ tablespoon salt

2 sticks butter, softened

Zest of 1 orange

2 to 3 tablespoons Grand Marnier

Powdered sugar for serving

In a saucepan, bring 2 cups water to a boil; whisk in flour and reduce heat to low. Cook 2 minutes and remove from heat. In the bowl of a stand mixer fitted with a whisk attachment, add egg yolks; set to high speed and whisk until yolks turn light in color. Add sugar and salt to yolks and continue whisking on high 2 minutes. In a bowl, combine egg yolk mixture with cooled flour mixture; add butter, orange zest and Grand Marnier. Mix thoroughly. Deep-fry ½-ounce portions of batter at 325° for 3 to 5 minutes or until evenly golden brown. Drain on paper towels. Dust with powdered sugar and serve while hot.

Restaurant Recipe

Roasted Corn Salsa

2 cups roasted (or grilled) fresh corn

1 green onion, sliced on bias

1 clove garlic, minced

1 jalapeño, diced

½ roasted red pepper, diced

1 teaspoon salt

1 teaspoon ground cumin

1 teaspoon chili powder

1 teaspoon finely chopped fresh cilantro

Salt and pepper to taste

Juice of 1 lime

In a mixing bowl, add all ingredients; fold together until evenly combined. Transfer to a serving bowl and serve with tortilla chips. Note: Roasting or grilling corn is optional but recommended; you may also use raw corn if desired, but be sure to let the salsa rest 15 to 20 minutes before serving.

Restaurant Recipe

Weidmann's Restaurant

210 22nd Avenue
Meridian, MS 39301
601-581-5770
www.weidmanns1870.com
Find us on facebook

When it comes to Meridian traditions, there are few quite as longstanding as having a wonderful meal at Weidmann's Restaurant. Since 1870, the restaurant has hosted generations of families around its tables, all to sample some of the greatest food and beverages available. Weidmann's has always specialized in high-quality comfort food prepared using the freshest ingredients, tried-and-true recipes, and a little bit of tender, loving care. Though the restaurant has changed hands over the years, the current owner, Charles Frazier, has continued to serve many of its original recipes along with new classics. Visit Weidmann's Restaurant for outstanding yet affordable Southern cuisine served in a historic setting.

Monday – Thursday: 11:00 am to 9:30 pm
Friday & Saturday: 11:00 am to 11:00 pm
JAZZ BRUNCH: Sunday: 10:00 am to 2:00 pm

Crab Dip

2 (8-ounce) packages cream cheese, softened

1 clove garlic

1 small onion, quartered

⅓ cup mayonnaise

1 teaspoon sugar

Dash salt

1 (6-ounce) can crabmeat, drained and flaked

¼ cup white grape juice

Assorted crackers for dipping

Combine cream cheese, garlic, onion, mayonnaise, sugar and salt in a blender; process until smooth. Add crabmeat and process in short bursts until meat is chopped but not puréed. Spoon into glass dish and microwave on medium 5 minutes or until heated through. Stir in grape juice. Serve with assorted crackers.

Local Favorite

Maple-Bacon Brussels Sprouts

4 slices thick-cut bacon, chopped

2 tablespoons butter

1 pound Brussels sprouts, trimmed and cut in half

3 tablespoons maple syrup

Salt and pepper to taste

Cook bacon in a cast-iron skillet over medium heat until crisp. Remove bacon from skillet and drain. Add butter to pan and melt. Add Brussels sprouts; cook, stirring occasionally until fork-tender. Add maple syrup. Crumble reserved bacon into pan. Cook another 30 to 60 seconds, stirring to coat the Brussel sprouts with syrup. Season to taste with salt and pepper.

Local Favorite

T-Bones, Too

113 South Main Street
Newton, MS 39345
601-357-5026
Find us on facebook

Welcome to T-Bones, Too, a restaurant serving the Newton community since May 2019. Most days, the eatery serves up diner classics, like burgers, sandwiches, and chicken tenders. Guests can also enjoy a variety of rotating daily specials such as homemade soups and plate lunches. On Sundays, T-Bones, Too offers a buffet, so you can get your fill of home-style fare at just the right price. Be sure to try the homemade desserts. Whether you want cheesecake, cake, pies, or cookies, they have it all and more. Pull up a chair at T-Bones, Too and see what all the fuss is about.

Tuesday – Friday: 11:00 am to 2:00 pm
Sunday: 11:00 am to 2:00 pm

Chicken Taco Casserole

4 cups shredded cooked chicken

2 (10.75-ounce) cans cream of chicken soup

1 (16-ounce) carton sour cream

1 (10-ounce) can Rotel tomatoes, drained

1 (15-ounce) can black beans, rinsed and drained

1 (1-ounce) envelope taco seasoning

5 cups crushed tortilla chips, divided

2 cups shredded Cheddar cheese, divided

Chopped lettuce, tomatoes, green onions and cilantro for garnishing

Preheat oven to 350°. Spray a 9x13-inch casserole dish with cooking spray; set aside. In a large bowl, stir together chicken, chicken soup, sour cream, Rotel, beans and seasoning. In prepared casserole dish, layer half of chicken mixture, 3 cups chips, and half of cheese. Layer remaining chicken mixture and chips. Cover dish with foil; bake 30 minutes. Uncover dish, top with remaining cheese and bake another 10 minutes uncovered. Top with lettuce, tomatoes, green onions and cilantro before serving.

Restaurant Recipe

15874 Highway 21
Sebastopol, MS 39359
601-625-7379
Find us on facebook

At Lee's Steakhouse, it's all about you. Lee's is a family-owned, family-oriented restaurant specializing in serving Premium Black Angus Beef. You'll feel at home the moment you pull up to the porch. They have a deep appreciation for their customers and to show it they keep their standards high. The menu is packed with hearty favorites from fried crawfish tails to grilled Atlantic salmon and shrimp and grits. They use Black Angus beef and cook your steak to absolute perfection. Finish off your meal with a slice of dessert and you'll be feeling full and happy.

Thursday:
4:30 pm to 8:30 pm
Friday – Saturday:
4:30 pm to 9:00 pm

Campers Dish

1½ pounds ground chuck
½ cup diced onions
Minced garlic to taste
2 (10.75-ounce) cans tomato soup
½ teaspoon oregano
1 tablespoon white vinegar
Salt and pepper to taste
2 cups cubed Cheddar cheese
1 (12-ounce) bag egg noodles, cooked

In a large saucepan over medium heat, brown meat. Add onion; cook until tender. Add garlic; cook 1 minute; drain. Add soup, oregano, vinegar, salt and pepper, then simmer. Add cheese and stir in egg noodles. Serve. Very quick dish all the kids will love.

Family Favorite

Grilled Whole Petite Green Beans

1 pound butter (or margarine; butter is better), divided

2½ pounds onions, sliced

5 pounds Polk's smoked sausage, sliced into medallions

½ pound bacon pieces

8 pounds fresh (or frozen) whole petite green beans

Salt and pepper to taste

Tony's Chachere's seasoning (or other seasoning salt) to taste

1 cup sugar

On a large flattop griddle, melt half butter and add onions. Sauté until translucent. Add sausage; sauté 3 to 5 minutes. Add bacon pieces. Spread the ingredients across the grill as evenly as possible. Add beans on top and let simmer 2 minutes. Slice and add remaining butter; toss the beans to mix. Add salt, pepper and Tony's, remembering to toss after adding. When beans are almost ready, sprinkle sugar evenly across top and toss. Simmer another 1 to 2 minutes, just enough time for the sugar to begin to caramelize. Carefully scoop beans into a serving pan and serve hot. This makes a large roasting pan of green beans.

Restaurant Recipe

Mac & Cheese

1 (16-ounce) package elbow macaroni

2 eggs, beaten

1 to 2 pints milk

Salt and pepper to taste

1 (8-ounce) package Velveeta (or Land of Lakes cheese)

2 cups grated smoked Cheddar cheese

2 cups grated mozzarella cheese

1½ stick of butter

Preheat oven to 350°. Cook macaroni in 2 quarts salted boiling water; drain. Grease 9x13-inch baking dish with butter or cooking spray. Using a large mixing bowl, mix eggs, milk, salt, and pepper; set aside. Slice Velveeta cheese evenly and spread across bottom of pan. Spread macaroni over cheese. Layer Cheddar, mozzarella and butter on top of macaroni. Carefully pour egg mixture over top just until you can see milk. Bake 1 hour or until the center bubbles and cheese on top browns slightly. Remove and serve.

Restaurant Recipe

The Little Dooey

100 Fellowship Street
Starkville, MS 39759
662-323-6094
www.littledooey.com
Find us on facebook

In 1985, Barry and Margaret Ann Wood opened The Little Dooey in Starkville, serving homemade barbecue and sauce out of a service station. The food was a hit, and soon the Wood family moved the business to its own restaurant to meet local demand. The restaurant was an instant success, and to this day, The Little Dooey remains Starkville's most popular barbecue joint, as voted on by the reader of the *Starkville Daily News*, *Mississippi Magazine* and the *Starkville Dispatch*. In addition to barbecue, guests can also enjoy salads, wraps, Mississippi farm-raised catfish, seafood, burgers, sandwiches, and more. All of their meats are flavored with the restaurant's signature rubs and slow-roasted to perfection. Visit The Little Dooey today and taste the pride of tradition.

Monday – Saturday: 11:30 am to 9:00 pm
Sunday: 10:30 am to 2:00 pm

Turnip Green Casserole Surprise

1 (16-ounce) package frozen turnip greens, cooked and drained
1 tablespoon prepared horseradish
1 (10.75-ounce) can cream of celery soup
½ cup mayonnaise
2 eggs, beaten
2 tablespoons red wine vinegar
1 tablespoon sugar
Breadcrumbs

Preheat oven to 350°. In a large bowl, mix together greens, horseradish, soup, mayonnaise, eggs, vinegar and sugar until combined. Transfer mixture to a greased 2-quart baking dish. Sprinkle breadcrumbs evenly over top. Bake 40 minutes or until golden brown. Serves 8.

Family Favorite

Gannie's Jalapeño Grits

1 cup quick-cooking grits
¼ ounce cream cheese
½ stick butter
1 (5-ounce) jar Old English cheese
¼ cup Worcestershire sauce
2 teaspoons chopped garlic
Garlic salt to taste
1 cup heavy cream
2 eggs, beaten
Finely diced jalapeños to taste

Preheat oven to 350°. Cook grits per directions on package; stir in cream cheese, butter and cheese until completely blended. Add Worcestershire, garlic and garlic salt. Fold in heavy cream until smooth. Stir in eggs until well blended. Stir in jalapeños to taste. Pour into a greased baking dish and bake until center is set.

Family Favorite

T-Bones Steakhouse

**10470 Highway 15 South
Union, MS 39365
601-774-9055
Find us on facebook**

T-Bones Steakhouse is the perfect place to grab a hot meal in a family-friendly environment. Weekdays, the lunch buffet features a parade of Southern-style classics that change each day. Enjoy fried fish, fried chicken, beef tips and gravy, turnip greens, baked beans, and much more. Guests can also order from a selection of choice steaks that are cut fresh and cooked to order. On Saturday nights, for a change of pace, T-Bones offers a seafood buffet that is fresh and hot. Oysters are also available as an add-on. Every other Saturday night, a gospel band plays live music as guests dine. Visit T-Bones Steakhouse for good food and good friends

Friday & Saturday:
5:00 pm to 9:00 pm
Sunday:
11:00 am to 2:00 pm

Spicy Grilled Potatoes

4 medium baking potatoes, washed
1 cup Italian salad dressing
1 teaspoon salt
¼ teaspoon pepper

Preheat oven to 400°. Bake potatoes 30 minutes. While potatoes are still hot, slice diagonally in ½-inch-thick slices; place in a shallow baking dish. Pour dressing over potatoes and let stand 1 hour. Remove potatoes and place on grill, 3 to 4 inches from hot coals. Grill 8 to 10 minutes on each side until brown. Season with salt and pepper.

Local Favorite

Rice Pudding

1½ cups cooked rice
¾ cup raisins
1 cup sugar
2 eggs, beaten
½ teaspoon vanilla
½ teaspoon cinnamon
Dash nutmeg
2 cups scalded milk
2 tablespoons butter, melted

In a bowl combine, rice, raisins, sugar, eggs, vanilla, cinnamon and nutmeg; mix well. Add milk and butter; mix well. Pour in buttered 9x9-inch casserole dish. Bake at 350° for 1 hour.

Local Favorite

Urban Country Kitchen

113 Main Street
Walnut Grove, MS 39189
601-253-2125
Find us on facebook

Urban Country Kitchen is a family-friendly establishment providing fresh meals made from scratch and filled with heart-felt love. Each dish is made using traditional family recipes handed down for generations. UCK takes pride in knowing each customer by name and guaranteeing that each plate prepared will "get you full." The staff at UCK takes pride in being active in the community and enjoys serving people using their new food truck. All you have to do is make the drive to 113 Main Street in Walnut Grove and they will handle the rest.

Thursday, Friday & Sunday:
11:00 am to 4:00 pm

Urban Country's Fried Chicken

Oil, for frying
1 cup hot red pepper sauce
2 cups self-rising flour
¼ cup black pepper, plus 1 teaspoon divided
1 (2½-pound) chicken, cut into pieces
1 cup salt
¼ cup garlic powder

In a deep fryer or a large heavy saucepan, heat oil to 350°. (Do not fill pot more than half full of oil.) In a medium-size bowl, combine 1 cup water and red pepper sauce; set aside. In another bowl, combine flour and ¼ cup pepper. Season chicken with remaining pepper, salt and garlic powder. Coat seasoned chicken in flour mixture and then dip into water mixture. Coat well in flour mixture again. Drop into oil, frying until golden brown.

Restaurant Recipe

Caramel Cake

Cake:

1 cup unsalted butter, softened

⅓ cup vegetable oil

2½ cups sugar

6 large eggs plus 2 large egg yolks, room temperature

1 cup sour cream

3 cups cake flour

1 teaspoon baking powder

½ teaspoon salt

2 tablespoons vanilla extract

Preheat oven to 350°. Spray 3 (9-inch) round cake pans with baking spray or grease and flour them; set aside. In a large mixing bowl, using an electric mixer, cream butter, oil and sugar on high 5 to 6 minutes or until light and fluffy. Turn mixer to medium speed; add eggs and egg yolks 1 at a time until well incorporated. Sift cake flour, baking powder and salt into medium-size bowl. With mixer on medium speed, alternately add flour mixture and sour cream ending with flour mixture. Add vanilla and beat until just mixed. Evenly divide batter between prepared pans. Bake 23 to 30 minutes or until toothpick inserted in center comes out clean. Remove cake pans from oven and cool on cooling racks 10 minutes. Remove cakes from pans and cool completely before icing.

Caramel Icing:

1½ sticks butter, softened

2 (12-ounce) cans evaporated milk

2 cups sugar

2 teaspoons vanilla extract

Using a large saucepan over medium heat, blend together butter, evaporated milk, and sugar until everything has melted together. Leave over medium to low heat stirring periodically about 1½ to 2 hours (watch the entire time to make sure it does not burn) until thickened and caramel has darkened to a beautiful golden brown. It should also thickly coat the back of a spoon to ensure thickness. Remove from heat and add vanilla. Cool about 15 minutes to allow it to thicken before icing the cake. If it is too warm and still not thick enough, cool in the refrigerator until thick. Once icing has cooled and thickened, frost each inner layer. Complete frosting the outside layers with the remaining icing.

Restaurant Recipe

CAPITAL

Brandon
Boo's Smokehouse Bar-B-Que 124
Fresh Market Café 126
Kismet's Restaurant 128

Brookhaven
Backwoods Bayou 130

Florence
Berry's Seafood & Catfish House 132
Jerry's Catfish House 134

Flowood
Eslava's Grille 136
Jo's Diner 138
Soul Sistas' Diner 140

Jackson
Aladdin Mediterranean Grill 142
Basil's 144
Brent's Drugs 146
The Iron Horse Grill 148
Keifer's Downtown 150
Martin's Downtown 152
Old Capital Inn 154
The Pig & Pint 156
Rooster's Restaurant 158

Madison
Mama Hamil's Southern Cooking & BBQ, Inc. 160
The Strawberry Café 162

Magee
Berry's Seafood & Catfish House 132

Mendenhall
Eason's Fish House 164
Smokey Mountain Grill & Rib Shack 166

Natchez
The Camp Restaurant 168
Cotton Alley Café 170

Pearl
Fresh Market Café 126
Moss Creek Fish House 172

Pelahatchie
CrawBilly's on the Tracks 174

Richland
Tom's Fried Pies 176

Ridgeland
Gumbo Girl 178

Tylertown
Black Dog Coffee & Café 180

Vicksburg
10 South Rooftop Bar & Grill 182
Anchuca 184
The Tomato Place 186
Walnut Hills Restaurant 188

2227 Highway 471
Brandon, MS 39047
601-829-0520
www.boossmokehouse.com
Find us on facebook

Welcome to Boo's Smokehouse Bar-B-Que, central Mississippi's premier barbecue restaurant. For years, Boo's Smokehouse has been providing locals and travelers from all corners of the world with tasty barbecue at fair prices. Enjoy pork butts smoked to perfection and pork steaks so tender you can cut right through them with a fork. Whether you're in search of lunch, dinner, or something to feed a crowd, Boo's Smokehouse has you covered. Be sure to stop in to taste the difference that freshness makes. Boo's Smokehouse Bar-B-Que is so good that you'll "hug the cook and kiss the pig"

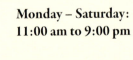

Monday – Saturday:
11:00 am to 9:00 pm

Buttermilk Pie

Boo's Grandmother's recipe

1½ cups sugar
1 stick butter, softened
2 tablespoons flour
3 eggs
1 teaspoon vanilla extract
½ cup buttermilk
1 (9-inch) frozen deep-dish pie crust

Preheat oven to 400°. In a bowl, cream together sugar and butter. Stir in flour and eggs. Stir in vanilla, then buttermilk. Pour filling into crust and place in oven; reduce oven to 350° and bake 40 to 45 minutes or until top of pie and crust is golden brown.

Family Favorite

Fresh Market Café

1877 Spillway Road
Brandon, MS 39047
601-919-8636

3029 Greenfield Road
Pearl, MS 39208
601-706-9981

www.jackiesinternational.com
Find us on facebook

Fresh Market Café opened its doors in 2002 with a simple concept: to provide Southern comfort food with a healthy twist. The vegetables are fresh or fresh frozen and cooked with chicken stock, ham base, and an in-house bacon and onion mix. You can also find a variety of homemade desserts that will remind you of a much simpler time like home-cooked meals that grandma used to make. The Fresh Market Café is convenient for families on the go, and moms can rest easy knowing that it's a healthy meal for the kids.

7 Days a Week:
11:00 am to 8:00 pm

Baked French Toast Casserole

1 loaf French bread, sliced
8 large eggs, beaten
2 cups half-and-half
1 cup milk
¼ cup sugar
1 teaspoon vanilla extract
¼ teaspoon cinnamon
¼ teaspoon nutmeg
Dash salt

Arrange bread slices in a generously buttered 9x13-inch baking dish. In a large bowl, combine eggs, half-and-half, milk, sugar, vanilla, cinnamon, nutmeg and salt. Beat vigorously with a whisk (or electric mixer) until mixed well. Pour over bread slices, making sure all are covered. Cover with foil and refrigerate overnight.

Pecan Topping:

2 sticks butter, melted
1 cup packed light brown sugar
1 cup chopped pecans
2 tablespoons light corn syrup
½ teaspoon cinnamon
½ teaspoon nutmeg

Preheat oven to 350°. Combine all ingredients in a medium bowl and mix well. Spread Pecan Topping evenly over bread; bake 40 minutes or until lightly browned.

Local Favorite

Ham Dogs

½ cup mayonnaise
1½ teaspoons chili powder
2 cups chopped ham
1½ cups shredded cheese
¼ cup chopped olives
¼ cup chopped green onions
Hot dog buns

In a bowl, mix mayonnaise and chili powder. Add remaining ingredients, except buns. Cover and cool 4 hours before serving. When ready to serve, spread mixture on hot dog buns; wrap in foil. Bake at 400° for 15 minutes.

Local Favorite

Kismet's Restaurant

**315 Crossgates Boulevard
Brandon, MS 39042
601-825-8380
Find us on facebook**

What started out as a favor to help a friend with her restaurant for a couple of months turned into a venture of a lifetime for Jackie Barnes and Jason Shepherd. Together they own the family-style restaurant that boasts of service excellence, Kismet's. The menu features gyros, po' boys, salads, sandwiches, and burgers with a variety of sides and appetizers all dolled up with Greek and Southern influences. Don't forget to visit during the Christmas season when the entire restaurant is decorated to include a varied collection of ornaments that hang from the ceiling.

Monday – Saturday:
11:00 am to 10:00 pm

No-Peek Chicken

1 whole chicken, cut up
2 cups Minute rice, uncooked
1 (2-ounce) package Lipton onion soup mix
1 (10.75-ounce) can cream of celery soup
1 (10.75-ounce) can cream of mushroom soup

Preheat oven to 350°. Grease a 9x13 casserole dish. Place chicken evenly in bottom. Mix together rice, soup mix, soups and 1 cup water. Pour over chicken. Cover tightly with foil and bake 2 hours. DO NOT PEEK.

Local Favorite

Ground Sirloin Dinner

2 pounds ground sirloin
7 to 8 medium-size potatoes, peeled and sliced
3 to 4 medium-size onions, sliced
1 (10.75-ounce) can cream of chicken soup
Salt and pepper to taste

Preheat oven to 350°. Form sirloin into patties and place in single layer in bottom of casserole dish. Alternate sliced potatoes with sliced onions in layers over meat. Pour soup, 1 soup can of water, salt and pepper over top. Bake covered 1 hour.

Local Favorite

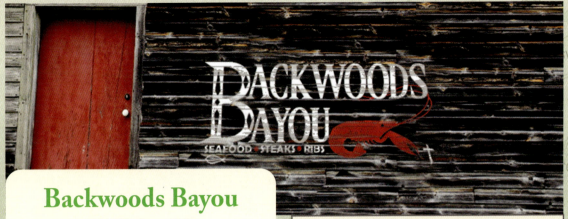

Backwoods Bayou

1811 Highway 550
Brookhaven, MS 39601
601-823-9749
Find us on facebook

Combining the best of Mississippi cuisine with a Cajun and Creole flair, Backwoods Bayou is ready to serve you an unforgettable, delicious meal. With an atmosphere constructed in a bayou motif, you get that Louisiana-style dining experience in an enchanting and comfortable setting without having to spend the extra gas money. Backwoods Bayou is famous for its steak and seafood menu items. From oysters to shrimp to catfish prepared grilled or fried, you're sure to find something to please your palate. Stop in at Backwoods Bayou for unique fare at reasonable prices.

Thursday – Saturday:
4:30 pm to 9:00 pm

Bay & Bayou

Best served smothered with your favorite crawfish étouffée and with salad and toasted Gambino French bread on side.

1 package Backwoods Bayou jambalaya mix (sold at Backwoods Bayou or can be shipped)

6 (3- to 5-ounce) flounder fillets

2 sticks butter

1 (16-ounce) can crab claw meat

1 teaspoon salt

1 teaspoon pepper

1 teaspoon cayenne pepper

Preheat oven to 350°. Cook jambalaya mix according to package directions. Put in 9x13-inch greased baking pan. Sauté flounder in butter to 100°. Place an equal amount of crab claw meat over each fillet and roll. Place on top of jambalaya. Sprinkle with salt, pepper and cayenne. Bake 15 minutes or to 140°.

Restaurant Recipe

Coke Cola Cake

Cake:

2 cups Coca-Cola
1 cup cooking oil
2 sticks butter
6 tablespoons cocoa
4 cups sugar
4 cups all-purpose flour
1 teaspoon salt
4 eggs, beaten
1 cup buttermilk
2 teaspoons baking soda
2 teaspoons vanilla

Preheat oven to 350°. In a saucepan over medium heat, bring cola, oil, butter and cocoa to a boil. Remove from heat; set aside. Using a medium mixing bowl, combine sugar, flour and salt. Pour cola mixture over flour mixture and beat well. Add eggs, buttermilk, soda and vanilla; beat well. Pour batter into a greased 9x13-inch baking dish. Bake until done. While cake is baking make frosting.

Frosting:

2 sticks butter
4⅔ tablespoons cocoa
12 tablespoons milk
7½ cups powdered sugar
2 teaspoons vanilla

In a saucepan over medium heat, combine butter, cocoa and milk. Heat until butter melts. Beat in remaining ingredients; mix well. Spread over cake while still warm. To serve, add marshmallows on top and toast 2 to 3 minutes on broil. Add ice cream, chocolate and caramel syrup on top.

Restaurant Recipe

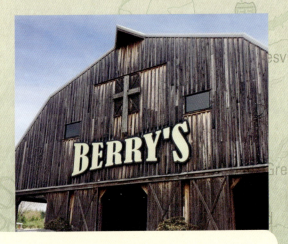

Berry's Seafood & Catfish House

2942 Highway 49 North
Florence, MS 39073
601-845-7562

1616 Highway 49 North
Magee, MS 39111
601-849-9313

www.berrysseafood.com
Find us on facebook

Berry's Seafood & Catfish House offers visitors a taste of the good ol' days with down-home cooking and the best seafood you'll find in their neck of the woods. Enjoy family dining where Southern hospitality is served by a waitstaff in overalls. While you are there don't forget to try Berry's signature Cajun sweet pickles served from a wheel barrow if you're brave enough to try 'em. Berry's has two locations to choose from, Florence and Magee, located on Highway 49.

Monday – Thursday: 10:30 am to 9:00 pm
Friday – Saturday: 10:30 am to 10:00 pm

Potato Pancakes

5 eggs, beaten
5 large potatoes, grated
2 tablespoons flour
½ teaspoon salt
3 tablespoons milk
Bacon fat (or butter)
Sugar, optional

In a large bowl, mix eggs and potatoes. Sift flour and salt into potato mixture; beat in milk. In a skillet over medium heat, heat bacon fat. Spoon 2 tablespoons batter per pancake into hot grease; cook 2 minutes per side, turning once. Serve immediately with butter and a sprinkling of sugar if desired.

Local Favorite

Skillet-Style Mexican Street Corn

1 tablespoon olive oil
4 cups fresh (or frozen) corn kernels, thawed if frozen
1 (10-ounce) can diced tomatoes with green chiles, drained
¾ cup grated pepper Jack cheese, divided
½ cup mayonnaise
Zest of 1 lime
¼ cup fresh cilantro leaves, coarsely chopped
Lime wedges for serving

Heat oil over medium heat in cast-iron skillet until it shimmers. Add corn and spread into an even layer. Cook 5 minutes stirring and smoothing back into an even layer until corn starts to brown. Add tomatoes and cook, stirring 1 minute. Add ½ cup cheese, mayonnaise and lime zest. Cook another minute stirring constantly. Stir in cilantro, top with remaining cheese. Serve with lime wedges.

Local Favorite

Jerry's Catfish House

3326 Highway 49 South
Florence, MS 39073
601-845-8860
Find us on facebook

Just off Highway 49 in Florence is a Mississippi marvel that most travelers would balk at: a giant white igloo that has withstood even the hottest Southern summers. The igloo is actually home to Florence's premier fried catfish outfit, Jerry's Catfish House. Patrons to Jerry's enjoy all-you-can-eat platters of tasty fried catfish for which the South is well known. Served with fries, hushpuppies, and Jerry's special coleslaw, catfish dinners don't get more Southern-style than that. The menu also features a variety of seafood choices, hamburger steaks, rib eyes, burgers, and even a few choice selections for diners with children. Visit today for a taste of this Florence tradition.

Thursday: 5:00 pm to 9:00 pm
Friday & Saturday: 4:00 pm to 9:30 pm
Sunday: 11:00 am to 8:00 pm

Catfish

Served with French fries, hushpuppies and cole slaw
Substitution available upon request:
Turnip greens, baked potato or baked sweet potato

All You Can Eat Catfish
No sharing allowed
No doggie bags
$16.95

Small Catfish Plate
Served with your choice
of 4 fillet or 1 whole
$12.95

Eslava's Grille

2481 Lakeland Drive
Flowood, MS 39232
601-932-4070
Find us on facebook

Danny "Danilo" Eslava was born and raised in Colombia. His roots and tradition for cooking and flavoring food started with his mother. When Danny moved to America, he and his family opened a restaurant called AJ's Seafood in the Jackson area, where Danny served as an award-winning head chef. Soon, he decided to open his own restaurant in Flowood. That restaurant is Eslava's Grille, serving up a mix of Colombian- and Cajun-influenced food. You'll love the flavor and casual yet relaxing atmosphere. Chef Danny wants his guests to be able to slow down for a moment, relax, and enjoy good food made from the heart.

LUNCH:
Monday – Friday: 11:00 am to 2:00 pm
DINNER:
Monday – Friday: 5:00 pm to 10:00 pm
Saturday: 5:00 pm to 10:30 pm

Salmon in Lemon Caper Sauce

Salmon fillets
Salt and pepper to taste
Oil
Heavy cream
Lemon juice
Capers
Eslava's seasoning (available in-house)

Season fillets with salt and pepper. In a medium-hot skillet, add oil and cook salmon. Remove salmon from skillet; set aside. In the same skillet over medium-low heat, add cream, lemon juice, capers and seasoning; reduce. Serve with angel hair pasta and sautéed vegetables.

Restaurant Recipe

Shrimp Scampi

Shrimp, peeled and deveined
Green onions, chopped
Tomatoes, diced
Garlic, minced
Eslava's seasoning (available in-house)
Heavy cream

In a skillet over medium heat, cook shrimp, onions, tomatoes, garlic and seasoning. Cover with heavy cream and reduce to thick sauce. Serve with pasta, rice or potatoes. For those allergic to seafood, substitute shrimp with cubed chicken breast.

Restaurant Recipe

Eslava's Sautée Zucchini and Squash

Oil
2 zucchini, sliced
2 squash, sliced
Green onions. sliced
Red tomatoes, diced
Eslava's seasoning (available in-house)

Heat oil in a skillet over medium heat. Add vegetables and seasoning. Cook, gently stirring, until vegetables are tender.

Restaurant Recipe

Jo's Diner

241 Ridge Way
Flowood, MS 39232
601-988-9000
www.josdiner.net
Find us on facebook

If you're looking for top-shelf cuisine with classic diner-style feel, look no further than Jo's Diner. This family-owned and family-operated restaurant has been serving the Flowood and Brandon communities since 2006. The menu features classic American breakfast options as well as lunch and dinner fare. Stopping by for breakfast? Try the Cajun Benedict, but don't leave without sampling the beignets. For lunch and dinner, guests can enjoy everything from blue plate specials to burgers and malts to milkshakes. The diner also offers a variety of salads, specialty sandwiches, pastas, and desserts. No matter when you visit, Jo's Diner has what you're craving.

Monday – Saturday: 7:00 am to 9:00 pm
Sunday: 7:00 am to 2:00 pm

Blueberry Cake

1 cup all-purpose flour
¼ cup packed brown sugar
1 stick margarine, softened
1 cup chopped pecans

Preheat oven to 350°. In a large bowl, mix all ingredients, using your hands, until well blended. Pat mixture into a 9x12-inch casserole dish. Bake 25-30 minutes or until browned on top; cool.

Filling:

2½ cups blueberries, washed
1 cup sugar
¼ cup all-purpose flour
1 tablespoon lemon juice

In a medium saucepan over low heat, simmer all ingredients until thickened; cool.

Topping:

1 cup whipping cream
6 ounces cream cheese, softened
¾ cup sugar
Vanilla extract to taste

In a large mixing bowl, beat whipping cream until soft peaks form. Add cream cheese, sugar and vanilla, continuing to beat until well blended. Place cake on a large platter and spread with filling. Top with cream mixture; chill and cut into squares to serve.

Local Favorite

Hot Breakfast Rolls

½ cup melted margarine
½ cup packed brown sugar
1 teaspoon cinnamon
1 (3.5-ounce) package butterscotch pudding mix (not instant)
1 (24-count) package frozen rolls
Nuts (or raisins) to taste

In a bowl, whisk together margarine, sugar, cinnamon, and pudding mix. Arrange rolls in a greased Bundt pan; pour mixture over rolls. Add nuts or raisins. Cover with a damp cloth; let rise overnight at room temperature. Bake at 400° for 15 to 20 minutes.

Local Favorite

Soul Sistas' Diner

690 Grants Ferry Road
Flowood, MS 39232
601-331-4892
Find us on facebook

Soul Sistas' is a family-owned and family-operated business that prides themselves in quality soul and comfort food. Everything is made fresh with love and soul in every bite. The menu features chicken, chili, sandwiches, wings, burgers, salads, and homemade sides. Don't forget to top it off with a big glass of sweet tea. Come hungry because Soul Sistas' will "Feed Ya Soul."

Monday – Thursday:
11:00 am to 8:00 pm
Friday & Saturday:
11:00 am to 9:00 pm

Impossible Taco Pie

The pie does the impossible by making its own crust.

1 pound ground chuck
½ cup chopped onion
1 (1.75-ounce) envelope taco seasoning mix
1 (4-ounce) can green chiles, drained
1¼ cups milk
¾ cup Bisquick baking mix
3 eggs, beaten
2 tomatoes, sliced
1 cup shredded Monterey Jack or Cheddar cheese

Preheat oven to 400°. Grease pie plate; set aside. In a skillet over medium heat, cook meat and onion until lightly browned; drain. Stir in seasoning mix. Spread in bottom of pie plate; top with chiles. Beat milk, Bisquick and eggs until smooth. Pour over meat. Bake 25 minutes. Top with tomatoes and cheese; bake another 10 minutes. Cool. May serve with sour cream, chopped tomatoes, shredded lettuce and shredded cheese.

Local Favorite

Apple-Raisin Slaw

2 medium Granny Smith apples, peeled and julienned
1 tablespoon lemon juice
½ small head cabbage, thinly sliced
¼ cup raisins
¼ cup mayonnaise
¼ teaspoon salt

In a large bowl, toss apples with lemon juice. Fold in cabbage, raisins, mayonnaise and salt. Mix well and serve.

Local Favorite

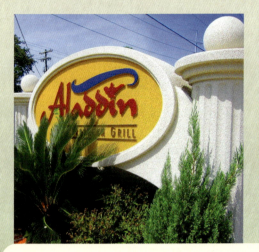

Aladdin Mediterranean Grill

730 Lakeland Drive
Jackson, MS 39216
601-366-6033
www.aladdininjackson.com
Find us on facebook

Located in Jackson near the historic Fondren Business District and UMMC, Aladdin Mediterranean Grill is the metro area's favorite spot for shawarma, gyros, baklava, and many other Mediterranean specialties. Experience the authentic flavors and elegance of Mediterranean cuisine, all made from scratch using fresh ingredients that speak to the simplicity, intensity, and richness of Mediterranean culture. Each plate is a feast for the eyes as well as the appetite. Whether you're looking for a dine-in family feast, a healthy meal on the go, or a delicious spread for your next event, Aladdin Mediterranean Grill has you covered

7 Days a Week:
11:00 am to 10:00 pm

Creamed Onions

¾ pound pearl onions
1½ cups White Sauce
½ cup breadcrumbs
½ cup melted butter

Preheat oven to 375°. Peel onions. Pierce each onion with a sharp knife or ice pick in center (this keeps them from coming apart while cooking). Place in a large amount of boiling salted water. Boil uncovered 15 minutes, or until tender. (Overcooking develops strong flavor and odor.) Place onions in a 4-quart casserole dish; cover with White Sauce. Combine breadcrumbs and butter; sprinkle on top. Bake 25 minutes or golden brown on top. Makes 4 to 6 servings.

White Sauce:

4 tablespoons butter
4 tablespoons flour
1 teaspoon salt
¼ teaspoon pepper
2 cups milk

Melt butter over low heat; add flour, salt and pepper. Stir until well blended. Gradually add milk, stirring constantly, until thick and smooth. Makes 2 cups.

Local Favorite

Baked Fish

1 teaspoon instant minced onion
½ teaspoon powdered mustard
¼ teaspoon crushed tarragon leaves
Pinch of pepper
1½ pounds flounder filets
Salt to taste
1 teaspoon lemon juice
½ cup mayonnaise
Paprika

Preheat oven to 425°. Combine onion, mustard, tarragon and pepper with 2 teaspoons warm water; set aside stand 10 minutes for flavors to blend. Dry fish and arrange in greased 9x11-inch glass baking dish; sprinkle with salt. Whisk in lemon juice and mayonnaise to tarragon mixture; spread over fish. Bake 25 to 30 minutes or until fish is browned and flakes easily. Garnish with paprika.

Local Favorite

Basil's

2906 North State Street
Jackson, MS 39216
601-982-2100
www.glennfoods.com
Find us on facebook

Basil's got its start in Jackson in 1984 as part of the Glennfoods family. The restaurant offers a clean Italian menu with paninis, pastas, and salads. All produce is delivered fresh daily and the bread is made hot and fresh every day. Catering is offered for any event and features their panini pies. Be sure to visit their sister restaurant, Rooster's of Fondren, while you are in the area.

Monday – Saturday:
11:00 am to 9:00 pm

Mississippi BACK ROAD RESTAURANT Recipes

Pan–Fried Kale

1 bunch kale, washed, dried, stems removed and coarsely chopped
4 large garlic cloves, roughly chopped
1 tablespoon olive oil
1 teaspoon salt, plus more to taste
2 tablespoons lemon juice
1 teaspoon red pepper flakes

Heat a cast-iron skillet on high 3 minutes. Add oil and garlic; cook 30 seconds. Add as much kale as will fit in pan along with salt. Using a set of tongs, turn kale in pan to wilt slightly. Add more kale in batches until all is added. Continue to cook 5 minutes or until kale is tender and garlic is fully cooked. Add lemon juice and red pepper, toss to coat. Add more salt if needed.

Local Favorite

Oyster Stew

2 tablespoons butter
1 pint fresh oysters
1 quart half-and-half
Salt to taste
Pepper to taste
Oyster crackers

In a saucepan over low heat, melt butter. Add oysters and their liquid. Cook 3 to 4 minutes until edges of oysters start to curl. Add half-and-half, salt and pepper; heat thoroughly but do not boil. Serve with crackers.

Local Favorite

Brent's Drugs

655 Duling Avenue
Jackson, MS 39216
601-366-3427
www.brentsdrugs.com
Find us on facebook

In October 1946, pharmacist Alvin Brent opened Brent's Drugs, a pharmacy and soda fountain, in the Fondren neighborhood. From the day the doors opened, Brent's enjoyed success, both as a pharmacy and as the neighborhood's unofficial gathering place. Over the decades, Brent's has largely remained the same charming diner it has always been, despite changes in ownership and a remodel in 2014. Brent's was even featured in Disney's 2011 film *The Help*. The pharmacy is no longer operational, instead it houses the diner's kitchen, but Brent's continues to prescribe soda fountain favorites and Southern hospitality. Stop in and enjoy a milkshake at the original 1946-era lunch counter with classic bar stools.

Monday: 7:00 am to 5:00 pm
Tuesday – Friday: 7:00 am to 8:30 pm
Saturday: 8:00 am to 8:30 pm
Sunday: 10:00 am to 3:00 pm

Brent's Chicken Salad

4 chicken breasts, boiled, drained and cooled
3 eggs, hard-boiled
½ red onion
2 celery stalks
¼ cup mayonnaise
1 teaspoon mustard
½ teaspoon salt
½ teaspoon pepper
Toasted bread, tomato slices and lettuce, optional
Crackers, optional

Chop chicken breasts into ¼-inch cubes; place in a large mixing bowl. Finely dice eggs, onion and celery and add to bowl with remaining salad ingredients; mix well. Serve Brent's Chicken Salad on toasted bread with tomato and lettuce or with crackers. Refrigerate up to 3 days.

Restaurant Recipe

Brent's Dreamsicle Shake

6 scoops orange sherbet
4 scoops vanilla ice cream
2 tablespoons vanilla simple syrup
4 tablespoons whipped cream, divided
2 maraschino cherries

Combine sherbet, ice cream and syrup in a blender; let sit 20 minutes to soften ice cream, then blend until smooth. Divide between 2 shake glasses and top each with 2 tablespoons whipped cream and 1 cherry. Enjoy

Restaurant Recipe

320 West Pearl Street
Jackson, MS 39203
601-398-0151
www.theironhorsegrill.com
Find us on facebook

Built as the Armour Smokehouse in 1906, this legendary Jackson landmark is a true icon of Mississippi's rich heritage. The old Iron Horse Grill burned down mysteriously twice. It was left abandoned after a fire in 1999. Fifteen years later it has been bought back up from the ashes like never before. The open kitchen and live music are the Mississippi way of living. The smell of charcoal greets you and the music pulls you inside. Be sure to check out the gift shop for Iron Horse apparel and Mississippi-made pepper jelly and pickles.

Monday – Wednesday: 11:00 am to 9:00 pm
Thursday: 11:00 am to 10:00 pm
Friday & Saturday: 11:00 am to 12:00 am
Sunday: 10:30 am to 3:00 pm

Caramel Apple Pecan Squares

1¾ cups flour
1 cup quick-cooking oats
½ cup packed brown sugar
½ teaspoon baking soda
½ teaspoon salt
1 cup cold margarine
1 cup chopped pecans
20 caramels, unwrapped
1 (14-ounce) can condensed milk
1 (21-ounce) can apple pie filling

Preheat oven to 375°. In a large bowl, combine flour, oats, sugar, baking soda and salt. Cut in margarine until crumbly. Add pecans to 1½ cups crumb mixture and set aside. Press remaining crumb mixture in bottom of a 9x13-inch baking pan. Bake 15 minutes. In a heavy saucepan over low heat, melt caramels and condensed milk, stirring until smooth. Spoon apple pie filling over baked crust. Top with caramel mixture and sprinkle reserved crumb mixture over top. Bake another 20 minutes or until set. Cool slightly. Serve warm with ice cream.

Local Favorite

Snowballs

5 tablespoons white corn syrup
3 tablespoons orange marmalade
2 tablespoons orange juice concentrate
1 (12-ounce) box vanilla wafers, finely crushed
48 mini marshmallows
1¾ cups sweetened coconut flakes

In a bowl, combine syrup, marmalade, and orange juice concentrate. Stir in crushed vanilla wafers and knead together until moistened and well mixed. Working with 2 mini marshmallows at a time, form mixture around the marshmallow into a 1-inch ball. Roll each ball in coconut to coat. Repeat, using all ingredients. Store in an airtight container up to 1 week.

Local Favorite

Keifer's DOWNTOWN

120 North Congress Street
Jackson, MS 39201
601-353-4976
www.keifersdowntown.com
Find us on facebook

Since 1981, Keifer's Downtown has been serving Jackson's favorite Greek food, with made-to-order sandwiches and quick, friendly service. Some of Keifer's specialties include gyros, hummus, and the famous feta dressing. The restaurant also offers extremely popular burgers and curly fries. Stop in today to see why Keifer's is downtown Jackson's favorite restaurant.

Monday – Friday: 11:00 am to 2:30 pm

White Chili

1½ pounds cooked chicken breast, shredded or diced

1 cup shredded Monterey Jack cheese plus more for serving

4 (15.5-ounce) cans great Northern beans

1 (14.5-ounce) can chicken broth

½ cup diced chile peppers

1 tablespoon garlic powder

1 teaspoon ground cumin

1 tablespoon chopped fresh oregano

Pinch ground cayenne pepper

Pinch ground cloves

1 onion, chopped

Salt and pepper to taste

Salsa for serving

In a soup cooker, combine all ingredients and simmer until beans are tender and chili is heated through. Serve topped with additional Monterey Jack and salsa.

Restaurant Recipe

Hummus

1 (16-ounce) can garbanzo beans

1 large lemon, juiced

Garlic powder to taste

⅓ cup tahini

Salt to taste

Chopped fresh parsley for garnish

Black olives for garnish

Paprika for garnish

Olive oil for topping

Pita bread chips for serving

In a food processor or blender, pulse beans with ¼ cup hot water until smooth. Transfer to a bowl; stir in lemon juice and garlic powder. In a food processor or blender, blend tahini with 1 tablespoon cold water; stir into bean mixture. Stir in salt. Serve topped with parsley, olives, paprika and a drizzle of olive oil, with pita on the side for dipping.

Restaurant Recipe

214 South State Street
Jackson, MS 39201
601-354-9712
www.martinsdowntownjxn.com
Find us on facebook

Martin's first got its start in 1953 when then owner, Martin Lassiter, opened the doors with a small grill and only served breakfast and lunch. In 1973 the restaurant moved and opened its doors as a bar serving beer only and brown-bagged the liquor, but there was one more move in store for Martin. Martin's was moved again in 1984 to the current location. Calvin Stodghill, Martin's friend, eventually took over as owner after Martin became ill in 1997. Since then the restaurant has been owned by Joseph Stodgill and has flourished tremendously with a new building and plenty of renovations. They now have a music venue added to the restaurant with daily blue plate specials and live music.

Monday – Saturday: 10:00 am to 2:00 am
Sunday: 10:00 am to 12:00 am

Three Cheese Pimento Cheese

1 (8-ounce) package cream cheese, softened
1 cup grated Parmesan cheese
4 cups shredded Cheddar cheese
⅓ cup Creole mustard
2 teaspoons lemon pepper
2 teaspoons dried parsley
2 tablespoons dehydrated onion
⅓ cup sour cream
⅔ cup mayo
1 (4-ounce) jar diced pimento
⅓ cup chopped jalapeno, optional

Add all to a mixing bowl; using an electric mixer, mix 2 to 3 minutes. Refrigerate 3 to 4 hours before use.

Restaurant Recipe

Lemon Butter Broccoli Parmesan

1½ sticks butter
Salt to taste
2 lemons juiced
2 teaspoons garlic salt
3 (12-ounce) packages frozen broccoli, cooked and drained
1 cup grated Parmesan cheese

Preheat oven to 350°. Using a small saucepan over medium heat, melt butter; add salt, lemon juice and garlic salt. Toss with drained broccoli. Pour broccoli into an 11x13-inch casserole dish; sprinkle with Parmesan cheese. Bake until warmed through.

Restaurant Recipe

Old Capitol Inn

226 North State Street
Jackson, MS 39201
601-359-9000
www.oldcapitolinn.com
Find us on facebook

The Old Capitol Inn welcomed its first guests in November of 1996. Due to the proximity to the Old Capitol Museum its name was born. The Inn features a New Orleans-style serenity garden, gala ballroom, and rooftop garden. Lunch is served in the sunroom or courtyard. The Old Capitol Inn is Jackson's premier location for receptions, proms, weddings, reunions, seminars, and a host of other activities.

Monday – Friday: 11:00 am to 2:00 pm

Blender Custard Pie

1 (12-ounce) can evaporated milk
3 tablespoons flour
3 eggs, beaten
1 cup sugar
3 tablespoons oil
½ teaspoon vanilla extract
Nutmeg (or cinnamon)

Preheat oven to 350°. In a blender, combine all ingredients except nutmeg. Mix just until flour is incorporated. Pour into greased and floured pie pan. Sprinkle with nutmeg. Bake 35 minutes or until knife inserted in center comes out clean.

Local favorite

Peanut Butter Fudge

2 cups sugar
2 tablespoons light corn syrup
⅔ cup milk
¼ teaspoon salt
1 teaspoon vanilla extract
½ cup peanut butter

In a cast-iron skillet, mix sugar, corn syrup, milk and salt. Cook over medium-high heat to soft-ball stage. Remove from heat; add vanilla and peanut butter. Beat 5 minutes and pour into a buttered dish. Cool until set and cut into squares.

Local Favorite

THE PIG & PINT

3139 North State Street
Jackson, MS 39216
601-326-6070
www.pigandpint.com
Find us on facebook

Located in the heart of Jackson, The Pig & Pint is an award-winning barbecue restaurant offering baby back ribs, brisket, nachos, tacos, and other creative takes on your favorite Southern classics. The restaurant serves Jackson and the surrounding communities awesome barbecue and one hundred kinds of craft beer with sides of nostalgia, a little flair, and warm and friendly Southern hospitality. Whether you try the barbecued chicken tacos with mango-jicama slaw, the pork belly corn dogs, or other menu highlights, The Pig & Pint will take your barbecue experience to the next level. Pair your meal with any of the one hundred craft beers and relax in a fun and family-friendly atmosphere. Come for the pig. Come for the pint.

**Monday – Saturday:
11:00 am to 9:00 pm**

Southern Cornbread

1½ cups cornmeal

1½ cups flour

1½ teaspoons baking powder

½ teaspoon baking soda

½ teaspoon salt

1½ cups buttermilk

3 large eggs, beaten

8 tablespoons bacon grease (or butter), divided

Place a 10-inch cast-iron skillet in oven and preheat to 400°. Using a mixing bowl, whisk together cornmeal, flour, baking powder, baking soda and salt. In another bowl, whisk together buttermilk, eggs and 6 tablespoons bacon grease. Add dry ingredients to wet ingredients and stir to combine. Carefully remove skillet from oven, add the remaining grease and swirl pan to coat. Pour in batter; cook 30 minutes or until golden brown. Cool in pan 5 minutes then turn out.

Local Favorite

Golden Brown Potatoes

¼ cup flour

Salt and pepper

¼ cup Parmesan cheese

5 large potatoes, quartered lengthwise

½ stick butter, melted

Preheat oven to 350°. In a shallow dish, combine flour, salt, pepper and cheese. Roll potatoes in flour mixture, then butter. Place on baking sheet. Bake 30 minutes. Rotate potatoes; bake another 30 minutes.

Local Favorite

Rooster's Restaurant

**2906 North State Street
Jackson, MS 39216
601-982-2001
www.glennfoods.com
Find us on facebook**

Rooster's, located at the heart of Fondren, got its start in 1984 and has served the Jackson area for over twenty-eight years. The restaurant is family oriented where you don't have to be afraid to bring the kids and let them eat. Rooster's is considered a classic Southern restaurant with its burgers, country fried steaks, and red beans and rice, always focusing on everything homemade and fresh including baked bread. They have many catering options from panini pies and burger bars to privately catered events, for a luncheon, meeting or office party.

**Monday – Saturday:
11:00 am to 9:00 pm**

Creole Tomato Gravy

2½ ounces butter

2½ ounces flour

½ cup diced celery

1 cup diced onion

2 cloves garlic, minced

½ cup diced carrots

6 cups chicken stock

1 cup whole, peeled, canned tomatoes, hand crushed

Salt and pepper to taste

1 rounded teaspoon oregano

In a skillet over medium heat, add butter and flour; cook stirring constantly to make peanut butter-colored roux. Add celery, onion, garlic and carrots; sweat 10 minutes. Add chicken stock and tomatoes. Cook 10 to 15 minutes or until thickened. Add salt and pepper. Stir well. Add oregano and serve.

Restaurant Recipe

Mama Hamil's Southern Cooking & BBQ, Inc.

751 Highway 51
Madison, MS 39110
601-856-4407
www.hamils.com
Find us on facebook

In 1977, the Hamil family opened Hamil's Restaurant with a fifty person seating capacity in a log cabin on a hill. The business plan was simple: feed hungry folks good food at a reasonable price. In 1994, Bob Hamil took over management of the restaurant. In 2007, Bob opened Mama Hamil's Southern Cooking & BBQ, Inc., at the current location, just behind that little log cabin. Mama Hamil's offers an in-house buffet of traditional Southern comfort food. The atmosphere is friendly and bustling The walls are decorated with history and reflect love of country, faith, and family. Stop on by and sample all the Southern delicacies they have to offer.

LUNCH:
Monday – Saturday: 10:30 am to 2:00 pm
DINNER:
Thursday – Saturday: 4:00 pm to 8:00 pm

Large Pound Cake

½ cup self-rising flour
2½ cups all-purpose flour
½ cup margarine, softened
1 cup Crisco shortening
3 cups sugar
6 eggs
1 cup milk
2 teaspoons vanilla

Preheat oven to 325°. Sift flours together 6 times; set aside. In a large bowl using an electric mixer, cream margarine, shortening and sugar well. Add eggs, 1 at a time; mix well. Add milk, vanilla and flours to creamed mixture; mix well. Pour batter into desired pan. Bake 1 hour and 20 minutes or until toothpick inserted in center comes out clean. NOTE: If you want to make it chocolate, add 1 (4-ounce) bar Baker's German sweet chocolate. Melt chocolate in a small saucepan with a tablespoon of water, stirring constantly. Pour into cake mixture.

Recipe from Ruthlene Hamil (Mrs. Bob)

Family Favorite

Williamsburg Orange Cake

2½ cups all-purpose flour
1½ cups sugar
1½ teaspoons baking soda
1½ cups buttermilk
¾ cup shortening
3 eggs
1½ teaspoons vanilla extract
1 cup golden raisins, chopped
½ cup chopped nuts
1 tablespoon grated orange peel

Preheat oven to 350°. In a large bowl using an electric mixer, mix all ingredients together and pour into 3 or 4 (9-inch) cake pans that have been greased and dusted with flour. Bake 30 to 35 minutes. Frost cake with Butter Frosting when cooled.

Butter Frosting:

½ cup butter, softened
4 cups powdered sugar
5 tablespoons orange flavor or orange juice
1 tablespoon grated orange peel

In a medium bowl, blend butter and sugar. Stir in juice and orange peel; beat until smooth. Frost cake between layers, sides and top.

Family Favorite

107 Depot Drive
Madison, MS 39110
601-856-3822
www.strawberrycafemadison.com
Find us on facebook

The Strawberry Café is a small, family-owned café serving lunch, boutique-style candlelit dinners, and Sunday brunch. Originally opened in 1987 as Madison's first restaurant, the café is currently owned by the Wade and Bach famillies, who bought and restored it in 2005. The Strawberry Café gets its name from Madison's history as a prominent strawberry producer, a local export that was then distributed by train from the very depot that houses the café today. In addition to rich history, the café has kept the traditional feel while offering a modernized menu by featuring healthy options and employing higher standards in food selection and preparation. Don't miss this landmark within a landmark.

Monday – Saturday: 11:00 am to 9:00 pm
Sunday: 10:30 am to 2:30 pm

Crab Chowder (Bisque)

⅔ cup olive oil
1 cup diced yellow onion
1 tablespoon minced garlic
1 cup diced green bell pepper
2 celery stalks, diced
½ cup diced green onion
2 tablespoons kosher salt
2 tablespoons black pepper
Pinch dried thyme
3 bay leaves
Pinch dried oregano
Dash cayenne pepper
1 teaspoon Old Bay seasoning
1 teaspoon Chef Paul Prudhomme's Blackened Redfish Magic seasoning
½ cup all-purpose flour
2 cups heavy cream
3 quarts milk
1 pound lump crabmeat

In a large stockpot, combine all ingredients except flour, cream, milk and crab; sauté over medium-high heat until vegetables are tender. Remove from heat and stir in flour until a paste forms. Stir in cream and return to medium-high heat. Stir continuously, touching but not scraping the bottom of the pot, until chowder is finished. Slowly add milk; after the first quart, add crab, then continue to add remaining milk slowly, stirring until soup reaches 185° and develops a thicker, frothy yet silky look. Taste for salt and adjust as needed.

By Chef Eric Bach

Restaurant Recipe

Sweet Potato Smash

6 sweet potatoes
½ pound butter, melted
½ teaspoon ground nutmeg
1 teaspoon ground cinnamon
½ teaspoon white pepper
1 teaspoon salt
½ cup sugar
½ cup packed brown sugar
1 cup heavy cream

Peel, cube and add sweet potatoes to a stockpot; cover with water and bring to a boil, cooking 20 minutes. When sweet potatoes are done, drain water and smash them with a potato masher. Whisk in butter, spices, seasonings and sugars until smooth. Whisk in cream until evenly distributed. Serve. Makes 2 quarts.

By Chef Eric Bach

Restaurant Recipe

Eason's Fish House

200 Merit Road
Mendenhall, MS 39114
601-847-2281
Find us on facebook

Drive on down to Eason's Fish House for catfish fried right. This Mendenhall staple is well known for being one of the best places around for serving up good old-fashioned Southern fried catfish. Guests can expect steaks, boiled crawfish, baked potatoes, salads of all kinds, smoked chicken, homemade hamburger steaks, burgers, rib eyes, and, of course, all-you-can-eat catfish. With exceptional service and so many tasty dining options, there's no wonder why Eason's Fish House is considered a jewel of the Mendenhall community.

Tuesday & Wednesday: 5:00 pm to 9:00 pm
Thursday – Saturday: 4:00 pm to 10:00 pm

Loaded Jalapeños

2 cups sliced jalapeños, breaded and fried

2 to 3 slices bacon, fried crisp and crumbled

Shredded Cheddar cheese for topping

Ranch dressing for topping

On a serving platter, arrange fried jalapeños. Sprinkle with crumbled bacon. Top with cheese as desired, then microwave until melted. Drizzle with ranch dressing and serve while warm.

Restaurant Recipe

Pulled Pork Baked Potato

1 russet potato, baked until tender

Prepared pulled pork for topping

Shredded Cheddar cheese for topping

Using a knife, split potato open lengthwise. Break up the inside a little with a fork, then fill middle of potato with pulled pork. Top with shredded cheese to taste. Microwave until cheese is melted. Serve warm.

Restaurant Recipe

Smokey Mountain Grille & Rib Shack

3799 Highway 49
Mendenhall, MS 39114
601-847-0340
Find us on facebook

If you're in the mood for Southern-style barbecue, you can't go wrong with Smokey Mountain Grille & Rib Shack. This Mendenhall restaurant serves up barbecue platters and plates, burgers, sandwiches, salads, and more. While you wait for your meal, enjoy some complimentary fresh-baked bread with honey butter. Regular diners recommend menu favorites like the pulled pork nachos and the Mighty Rib platter. Smokey Mountain Grille & Rib Shack awaits your visit.

LUNCH:
Tuesday – Friday: 11:00 am to 2:00 pm
DINNER:
Thursday & Friday: 5:00 pm to 9:00 pm
ALL DAY SATURDAY:
11:00 am to 9:00 pm

Jalapeño Jelly

13 cups sugar
3 cups apple cider vinegar
2 tablespoons lemon juice
1½ cups chopped jalapeño
1½ cups chopped bell pepper

In a heavy-bottom pot over medium heat, mix all ingredients. Cook until mixture comes to a boil. Let boil 2 minutes and turn heat off. Ready to put in jars.

Restaurant Recipe

Baked Bean Base

2 pounds bacon, chopped
½ cup butter-flavor oil
1 pound onions, chopped
1 pound bell peppers, chopped
3 tablespoons ham base
8 cups brown sugar
4 cups B-B-Q Rub

In a large stockpot over medium heat, cook bacon in oil. Add onions and peppers; cook until tender. Add ham base, sugar and rub; cook until sugar has dissolved.

Restaurant Recipe

Smoked Chicken Salad

2 pounds pulled smoked chicken
½ cup chopped onion
½ cup Smokey Mountain Grill rub (available in-house)
1 cup sweet pickle relish
4 cups mayonnaise

Using a large bowl, mix all ingredients together. Serve on toasted homemade bread topped with lettuce and tomato.

Restaurant Recipe

The Camp Restaurant

21 Silver Street
Natchez, MS 39120
601-897-0466
Find us on facebook

Located in the historic "Under-the-Hill" district in downtown Natchez, The Camp Restaurant is a local gathering place for friends and family. At The Camp, you'll enjoy good comfort food, live sports television, wonderful beer, and the chance to share stories. The menu features everything from burgers to melts to fried platters to tacos. Enjoy your meal on the porch overlooking the mighty Mississippi River or in front of one of the many flat-screen TVs if you're looking for a little more excitement. Whatever you choose, you're sure to have a good time at The Camp Restaurant.

Sunday – Thursday: 11:00 am to 9:00 pm
Friday & Saturday: 11:00 am to 10:00 pm

Brisket Rub

1 cup packed brown sugar
½ cup paprika
½ cup salt
½ cup ground black pepper
2 tablespoons garlic powder
1 tablespoon ground cumin
1 tablespoon ground cinnamon

In a bowl, combine all ingredients and mix until even distributed. When ready to use, rub down brisket; refrigerate several hours so flavors can penetrate meat. Store extra in an airtight container.

Restaurant Recipe

Bloody Mary

2 ounces Tito's handmade vodka
2 (5.5-ounce) cans tomato juice
½ teaspoon celery salt
½ teaspoon seasoned salt
½ teaspoon Tony Chachere's original Creole seasoning
¾ ounce Worcestershire sauce
½ teaspoon horseradish
2 dashes Tabasco hot sauce
1 lemon wedge
1 lime wedge
1 Bloody Mary skewer (1 pickled bean, 1 olive, 1 pickled okra) for garnish

In a serving glass, combine vodka, juice, salts, seasoning, Worcestershire, horseradish and Tabasco. Squeeze lemon and lime wedges into glass, then stir with a spoon. Add ice as desired, then garnish with lemon and lime wedges and skewer.

Restaurant Recipe

Sweet Heat BBQ Sauce

1 (114-ounce) can ketchup
2 cups molasses
½ cup Colman's dry mustard
2 tablespoons liquid smoke
1 cup apple cider vinegar
½ cup red chili flakes
6 (11.2-ounce) bottles Guinness beer

In a large stockpot, combine all ingredients over medium heat and cook, stirring constantly, until bubbling and slightly reduced. Refrigerate in an airtight container.

Restaurant Recipe

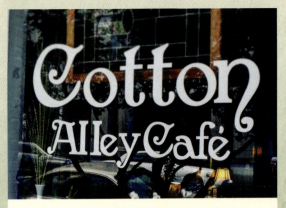

208 Main Street
Natchez, MS 39120
601-442-7452
www.cottonalleycafe.com
Find us on facebook

Welcome to Cotton Alley Café, a charming destination tucked away in cozy Natchez, right on the Mississippi River. It's a well-known fact that cafés bring people together, and Cotton Alley is no exception. Whether you visit for a pleasant afternoon or a romantic evening, with friends and family or on official business, Cotton Alley has a mouth-watering meal in store for everyone. With a great selection of sandwiches and salads for lunch and pasta dishes, steaks, and grilled fish for dinner, you'll have a hard time choosing from so many delicious options. Don't forget to ask about the daily special. Eclectic and quaint, Cotton Alley Café has it all.

LUNCH:
Monday – Saturday: 11:00 am to 2:00 pm
DINNER:
Monday – Saturday: 5:30 pm to 9:00 pm

Chicken and Tasso

1 (6-ounce) boneless, skinless chicken breast
Olive oil for cooking
¼ cup chopped green onion
¼ cup sliced mushrooms
½ tablespoon chopped garlic
¼ cup chopped tasso
1 teaspoon Tony Chachere's seasoning

Cook chicken breast and set aside. In a skillet with a small amount of olive oil, sauté green onion, mushrooms, garlic, tasso and seasoning until warmed through. Add chicken and Cream Sauce.

Cream Sauce:

6 ounces cream cheese, softened
2 tablespoons butter
¼ cup Parmesan cheese
1 cup half-and-half

Using a small saucepan over medium low heat, cook to desired thickness. If too thick add more half-and-half. Use in above recipe or pour over your favorite pasta.

Restaurant Recipe

Pasta Salad

1 cup sliced green onions
1 cup sliced black olives
1 cup sliced green salad olives
1 cup chopped red bell pepper
1 cup chopped purple onion
1 cup whole black olives
1 cup chopped cucumber
1 cup chopped pear tomatoes
¼ cup capers, chopped
1 (16-ounce) jar Boscoli olive mix or any good olive mix
¼ cup olive oil
3 quarts cooked penne pasta
Granulated garlic to taste
Black pepper to taste
2 cups grated Parmesan cheese

In a large bowl mix all ingredients except cheese. Add cheese. Refrigerate and serve cold.

Restaurant Recipe

413 Riverwind Drive
Pearl, MS 39208
601-932-7424
www.mosscreekfishhouse.com
Find us on facebook

Welcome to Moss Creek Fish House, a family-owned and family-operated restaurant serving Pearl and the surrounding communities since July 2012. At Moss Creek, the staff take pride in the business and make it their purpose to serve customers nothing short of delicious food as well as great customer service. Be sure to sample the catfish, which is farm raised in the United States and sure to please. You're sure to enjoy everything Moss Creek Fish House has to offer, so sit back, relax, and dig in

Monday – Saturday: 10:30 am to 9:00 pm
Sunday: 10:30 am to 8:00 pm

Mashed Potato Casserole

2 tablespoons plus 1 teaspoon salt, divided

6 pounds Yukon gold potatoes, peeled and cut into chunks

14 tablespoons butter plus more for preparing dish, divided

1½ cups sour cream

2 large eggs beaten

Pepper to taste

6 tablespoons finely chopped chives

⅔ cup Panko breadcrumbs

½ cup Parmesan cheese

Preheat oven to 400°. In a large stockpot, combine 4 quarts water, 2 tablespoons salt and potatoes. Bring to a boil, cook 20 minutes or until potatoes are fork-tender. Drain potatoes, return to pot and cook, stirring until potatoes stop steaming. Grease a Dutch oven with butter. Mash the potatoes with 10 tablespoons butter, sour cream, eggs, 1 teaspoon salt and pepper. Stir in the chives. Spread the potatoes into Dutch oven. Melt the remaining tablespoons butter and combine with breadcrumbs and cheese. Sprinkle cheese mixture over top. Bake 30 to 40 minutes or until golden brown.

Local Favorite

Greek Coleslaw

1 medium head cabbage, shredded

1 carrot, thinly shredded

½ cup olive oil

¼ cup chopped fresh parsley

1 clove garlic, chopped

1 teaspoon oregano

2 lemons, juiced

Salt and pepper to taste

In a large mixing bowl, toss together cabbage and carrot; set aside. Using a food processor, blend oil, parsley, garlic, oregano and lemon juice; add salt and pepper to taste. Add to cabbage-carrot mixture mixing well. Enjoy

Local Favorite

CrawBilly's on the Tracks

109 1st Street
Pelahatchie, MS 39145
601-316-9801
Find us on facebook

Located in Pelahatchie, CrawBilly's is a great place to eat delicious food, enjoy music, and relax with friends and family just a few yards from the tracks. The menu features Philly cheese steaks, po' boys, shrimp, hand-battered onion rings, steak, pistolettes, boiled crawfish, and so much more. There's also an occasional musical saw show, a fire pit, a back deck, and even a giant tree smack dab in the middle of the restaurant. If you're looking for scrumptious food in a great atmosphere, look no further than CrawBilly's on the Tracks.

Thursday: 4:00 pm to 9:00 pm
Friday: 11:00 am to 1:30 pm;
4:00 pm to 9:00 pm
Saturday: 11:00 am to 9:00 pm

Bacony Baked Beans

1 (1-pound) bag dry
great Northern beans
6 slices thick-cut bacon, chopped
1 large white onion, diced
1 jalapeño, seeded, deveined
and minced
1 cup barbecue sauce
¼ cup packed light brown sugar
¼ cup ketchup
¼ cup apple cider vinegar
1 teaspoon dry mustard

Place beans in a large bowl, cover with water; soak overnight. Drain, rinse and place beans in Dutch oven. Cover with fresh water; bring to a boil. Reduce heat, cover and simmer 2 hours. Drain the beans. Preheat oven to 325°. Rinse pot, put back on stove over medium heat. Add bacon and cook, stirring occasionally, until cooked through but not crispy. Add onion; cook 5 minutes or until tender, stirring occasionally. Add jalapeño; cook an additional 1 minute. Add beans back to pot along with remaining ingredients. Cook while stirring 2 to 3 minutes. Put lid on pot and bake 2 hours or until the sauce is the consistency of syrup. Let rest a few minutes before serving.

Local Favorite

Barbecued Spareribs

2 tablespoons Worcestershire sauce
1 tablespoon wine vinegar
1 tablespoon thick meat sauce
1 tablespoon sugar
¼ cup ketchup
Dash hot sauce
2 to 3 pounds spareribs

Combine Worcestershire, vinegar, meat sauce, sugar, ketchup and hot sauce in a bowl; whisk thoroughly. Cook spareribs over hot charcoal 2 hours or until tender, turning frequently. Cook, turning and basting with prepared sauce frequently, another 15 minutes. Enjoy.

Local Favorite

Tom's Fried Pies

www.tomsfriedpies.com • (769) 257-7351
827 Hwy 49 S, Richland, MS 39218

827 Highway 49 South
Richland, MS 39218
769-257-7351
www.tomsfriedpies.com
Find us on facebook

Tom's Fried Pies was inspired by his Mama, Ms. Lillie. Back in the day she made her husband fried pies for his lunch in the coal mines of Kentucky. He noticed his pies would come up missing when he stopped to eat. The other miners all wanted Ms. Lillie's pies. She began to take orders and send pies. Today is no different. Everyone wants to eat a good fried pie. Fruit, cream, and meat pies are now available for you to enjoy. Tom's was named one of the "TOP 10" places in America to get the best apple pie. If you are really hungry, they also offer special prices by the dozen.

Tuesday – Saturday:
10:00 am to 7:00 pm

Mallory's Banana Pudding

1 (5.1-ounce) box instant vanilla pudding

1 (3.4-ounce) box instant vanilla pudding

5 cups almond milk

1 (14-ounce) can Eagle brand condensed milk

5 bananas sliced in rounds

1 (8-ounce) carton light Cool Whip

1 (11-ounce) box mini vanilla wafers

In a large bowl, mix together puddings, almond milk and condensed milk. Add bananas and fold in Cool Whip. Gently fold in vanilla wafers.

Family Favorite

Breakfast Casserole

½ stick butter

6 slices white bread, crust removed

1 pound sausage, cooked and drained

1½ cups shredded Cheddar cheese

5 eggs, well beaten

2 cups half-and-half (or 1 cup evaporated milk and 1 cup 2% milk)

1 teaspoon salt

1 teaspoon dry mustard

Melt butter in a 9x13-inch casserole dish. Tear bread in small pieces; spread over butter. Sprinkle sausage over bread. Sprinkle cheese over sausage. In a large bowl, beat eggs with remaining ingredients; pour over casserole. Chill 8 hours or overnight. Preheat oven to 350°. Bake 40 to 50 minutes.

Family Favorite

Kayla's Homemade Ice Cream

2 (14-ounce) cans sweetened condensed milk

1 pint half-and-half (or 2 [12-ounce] cans evaporated milk)

2 teaspoons vanilla extract

Whole milk

In a large bowl, combine condensed milk, half-and-half and vanilla. Make sure ingredients are well mixed. Pour mixture into ice cream freezer container. Pour whole milk up to fill line of container. Freeze as you normally would.

Family Favorite

Capital

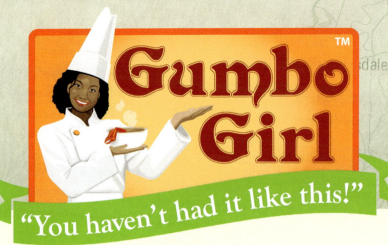

Gumbo Girl

"You haven't had it like this!"

900 East County Line Road, Suite 107
Ridgeland, MS 39157
601-790-0486
www.gumbogirl.com
Find us on facebook

Gumbo Girl serves the best gumbo in town. Surf-n-Turf Gumbo is a customer favorite. Seafood lovers and Pescatarians, enjoy the All Seafood Gumbo. For those allergic to shellfish, enjoy Chicken and Sausage Gumbo. For non-meat eaters, there is Vegetarian Gumbo that Vegans enjoy as well. The menu is well-rounded and touches on other favorites such as red beans and rice, burgers, and tacos. As well as jambalaya, shrimp and crawfish etouffee, shrimp Alfredo, and seafood creamy garlic pastas. Whether it's a game day, birthday party, business luncheon, or just a regular visit, great quality, great food, and great times are to be had.

Tuesday – Friday: 11:30 am to 8:00 pm
Saturday: 3:00 pm to 8:00 pm

Cajun Red Beans and Rice with Sausage

1 pound dry kidney beans
1 large onion, chopped
3 cups chopped green onions
1 green bell pepper, chopped
2 stalks celery, chopped
¼ cup olive oil
4 bay leaves
2 tablespoons salt
1 tablespoon Cajun seasoning
1 diced jalapeño pepper
1 pound Cajun sausage, cut in rounds

In a large stockpot over medium heat, cook beans in 6 cups water. Cook about 2 hours, checking to make sure water is always over beans, add water as needed. In a skillet over medium heat, sauté onions, bell pepper and celery in oil; add to stockpot. Add bay leaves, salt, seasoning, jalapeno and sausage to pot; cook another hour or until flavors meld and sausage is tender.

Restaurant Recipe

Homemade Sweet Cornbread

¼ cup oil
2 cups cornmeal
1 cup flour
1 cup sugar
1½ cups milk
2 eggs, beaten
1 stick butter, melted

Preheat oven to 425°. Add oil in cast-iron skillet; place in oven to preheat. Using a large mixing bowl, combine remaining ingredients: pour into skillet. Bake 25 minutes or until cornbread is browned on top.

Restaurant Recipe

711 Beulah Avenue
Tylertown, MS 39667
601-310-3465
www.black-dog-coffee-cafe.business.site
Find us on facebook

Black Dog Coffee & Café is a vision become reality. Ernie Whittington and Lisa Mathews dreamed of opening their own coffee house and café for most of their lives. That dream came true in September 2017 when the friends opened Black Dog Coffee & Café. The name is inspired by Ernie's black lab, Fred, and his unconditional love for all things. The Black Dog serves up salads, sandwiches, po' boys and more, in addition to Mississippi-roasted coffee sourced right out of Hattiesburg. Come enjoy the warm, cozy atmosphere and phenomenal treats that make Black Dog Coffee & Café a Tylertown staple.

Monday – Thursday: 7:00 am to 2:00 pm;
5:00 pm to 8:00 pm
Friday: 7:00 am to 2:00 pm
Saturday: 8:00 am to 1:00 pm

Luscious Potato Casserole

2 cups cottage cheese
1 cup sour cream
⅓ cup sliced green onions
1 clove garlic, minced
2 teaspoons salt
5 cups cubed cooked potatoes
½ cup shredded Cheddar cheese
Paprika

Preheat oven to 350°. In a large bowl, combine cottage cheese, sour cream, onions, garlic and salt. Fold in potatoes. Pour into a greased 1½-quart casserole dish, top with cheese and sprinkle top with paprika. Bake 40 minutes.

Local Favorite

Meatloaf

1½ pounds ground beef
16 saltine crackers, crushed
1 (8-ounce) can tomato sauce, divided
1 egg, beaten
1 teaspoon salt
¼ teaspoon pepper
1 tablespoon minced onion
1 tablespoon Worcestershire sauce
½ teaspoon seasoned salt
½ teaspoon dry mustard
¼ teaspoon garlic salt
½ cup ketchup

Preheat oven to 350°. Mix together meat, crackers, ½ can tomato sauce, egg, salt, pepper, onion, Worcestershire, seasoned salt, mustard and garlic salt. Form into 2 loaves and place in a lightly greased 9x13-inch baking dish. Pour remaining tomato sauce over each loaf, loosely cover dish with foil and bake 30 minutes. Remove from oven; spread ketchup over tops and bake another 30 minutes.

Local Favorite

10 SOUTH
ROOFTOP BAR & GRILL

1301 Washington Street, 10th Floor
Vicksburg, MS 39180
601-501-4600
www.10southrooftop.com
Find us on facebook

Established in 2015, 10 South Rooftop Bar & Grill is a relaxed restaurant and bar located on the rooftop of the First National Building in downtown Vicksburg. The menu features a variety of sandwiches, salads, chicken and seafood plates, and for those with a sweet tooth, a selection of scrumptious desserts, like Salted Caramel Brûlée. 10 South also offers a wide selection of to-go Drinks that serves two to four people. As if a delicious meal and cold refreshments weren't enough, guests also have the option to sit indoors or dine outdoors on the terrace overlooking the beautiful Mississippi River.

Sunday, Tuesday — Thursday:
5:00 pm to 9:00 pm
Friday & Saturday:
4:00 pm to 10:00 pm

10 South Comeback Sauce

Can be used as a dip for vegetables, as salad dressing, seafood sauce and sandwich spread.

1 tablespoon oil
2 celery stalks, diced
1 yellow onion, diced
1 red bell pepper, diced
1 tablespoon garlic purée
1 tablespoon Creole mustard
1 cup Duke's mayonnaise
3 tablespoons lemon juice
2 tablespoons Old Bay seasoning
1 teaspoon pepper
1 teaspoon Tabasco sauce
1 teaspoon Worcestershire sauce
1 teaspoon salt

In a small saucepan over medium heat, add oil; sauté celery, onion, and pepper 3 to 5 minutes until translucent. Add garlic; sauté 1 minute. Remove from heat. Combine all ingredients in a blender, blending until smooth. Store in air tight container. Serve over crab cakes.

Restaurant Recipe

10 South Crab Cakes

1 tablespoon butter
½ cup minced onion
½ cup minced celery
½ cup minced red bell pepper
1 teaspoon chopped garlic
2 eggs, beaten
½ cup Duke's mayonnaise
1 tablespoon Creole mustard
1 tablespoon chopped parsley
¼ teaspoon Louisiana hot sauce
½ teaspoon Worcestershire sauce
2 teaspoons Old Bay seasoning
½ teaspoon pepper
¼ teaspoon salt
½ cup panko breadcrumbs
1 pound crabmeat
1 tablespoon oil

Melt butter in saucepan over medium heat. Sauté onions, celery, and peppers until translucent. Add garlic; cook 1 minute. Using a mixing bowl, combine eggs, mayonnaise, mustard, parsley, hot sauce, Worcestershire, cooked vegetables, seasonings and breadcrumbs. Gently fold in crabmeat so crabmeat stays intact. Refrigerate at least 30 minutes. Shape patties to desired size. In a nonstick skillet, heat oil; sauté crab cakes until golden brown.

Restaurant Recipe

ANCHUCA
— CIRCA 1830 —

1010 First East Street
Vicksburg, MS 39183
601-661-0111
Find us on facebook

Anchuca first opened as a historic mansion and inn. Through the years the restaurant was born. The café offers a casual yet elegant dining experience offering award-winning gourmet Southern dishes. The Sunday brunch is a local's favorite and a must-do for tourists. Stop in for dinner where the Café Fillet is featured and said to be so tender you won't need a steak knife. Other specialties include a scrumptious Shrimp & Grits, Paneed Catfish, and the very popular Surf & Turf, a proven people pleaser. Top off your dining experience with one of their heavenly homemade desserts.

Monday – Saturday:
5:00 pm until Closing
Sunday:
11:00 am to 2:00 pm

Anchuca Bonzo Recipe
Cake:
1¼ sticks butter, softened

1 (12-ounce) package semisweet chocolate chips

6 large eggs, separated

⅔ cup sugar

Preheat oven to 350°. Spray a 9-inch springform pan with baking spray; wrap in foil to keep batter from leaking. Using a double boiler over medium heat, melt butter and chocolate chips. Set aside to cool. Place egg yolks in bowl and whisk in sugar until well combined. Using an electric mixer, beat egg whites until fluffy and soft peaks form. Add chocolate mixture to sugar mixture, whisking to blend well. Carefully fold this mixture into egg whites just until blended. Pour batter into pan; tap to remove air bubbles. Bake 40 minutes or until toothpick inserted in center comes out clean. Transfer to rack to cool completely. As cake cools center will sink, press down sides to match evenness. While cake is cooling make ganache:

Ganache:

1 cup semisweet chocolate chips
½ cup plus ⅓ cup whipping cream
2 tablespoons butter, softened
1 tablespoon Kahlua coffee-flavored liqueur

Using a food processor, chop chocolate chips fine. Heat cream just until boiling and pour into tube of processor in a slow steady stream with motor running. Add butter and liqueur; process until smooth. Pour ganache over cooled cake to form a ½-inch layer. Refrigerate at least 1 hour. Make filling.

Cream Cheese Crostata Filling:

1½ (8-ounce) packages cream cheese, softened
1 cup mascarpone cheese
⅔ cup sugar
1½ tablespoons Amaretto almond liqueur

In a large bowl, beat cheeses together until light and fluffy. Add sugar and liqueur, scraping the bowl often. Spoon mixture evenly over cooled ganache, being careful not to mix the 2 layers. Cool 1 hour before adding Chocolate Mousse.

Chocolate Mousse:

1 (12-ounce) package chocolate chips
1 (8-ounce) package cream cheese, softened
¼ cup strong coffee, room temperature
¼ cup Grand Marnier orange liqueur
1 cup Cool Whip

Melt chocolate chips in a double boiler; cool. Using an electric mixer, beat cream cheese until light and fluffy. Add chocolate and beat until smooth. Turn mixer on lowest speed; slowly add coffee and liqueur and combine before building speed. Fold in Cool Whip until just combined. Carefully spoon mousse over crostata mounding higher in center. Refrigerate at least 4 hours before serving. May top with extra Cool Whip, chocolate syrup and caramel syrup.

Restaurant Recipe

The TOMATO PLACE

3229 Highway 61 South
Vicksburg, MS 39180
601-661-0040
www.thetomatoplace.com
Find us on facebook

The Tomato Place is an old-timey fruit stand that tries to capture the quality, flavor, and personality of years gone by. Established in 2001, The Tomato Place serves up home-cooked food, real fruit smoothies, fresh-squeezed lemonade, and fresh-brewed iced tea. Visitors rave about the BLTs made with fresh tomatoes. Fresh-baked cookies, cakes, candies, and pies are made from scratch daily. The Tomato Place also offers plants, art, music, and handcrafted gifts that make this roadside stand one of a kind.

Open 7 Days a Week:
8:00 am to 8:00 pm

Chocolate Bread Pudding

Stale bread (enough to fill a 9x13-inch baking pan)
4 eggs
2⅔ cups sugar
14 tablespoons cocoa powder
4 cups milk
2 teaspoons vanilla extract

Preheat oven to 350°. Break bread into small pieces and fill a 9x13-inch baking pan. In a bowl, mix eggs, sugar, cocoa, milk and vanilla; pour over bread and allow to soak it up. Bake 1½ hours or until firm.

Sauce:

2 sticks softened butter
2 cups powdered sugar (or 1 cup sugar)
1 tablespoon milk

In a bowl, mix together all ingredients until combined. Pour over warm Chocolate Bread Pudding and serve.

Restaurant Recipe

Tomato Place Pie

2½ cups Italian breadcrumbs, divided
2 (8-ounce) packages sliced sharp Cheddar cheese, divided
6 large tomatoes, peeled and sliced
1 onion, sliced into rings
8 slices bacon, cooked and crumbled
¾ cup bacon-ranch dressing
¾ cup mayonnaise
Salt and pepper
1½ cups cottage cheese
2 tablespoons dried oregano
1 green bell pepper, sliced

Preheat oven to 350°. In a 9x12-inch baking dish, spread 1 cup breadcrumbs and layer half of Cheddar over top. Layer a third of tomato slices, onion to taste and a third of bacon. In a bowl, combine bacon-ranch dressing and mayonnaise; spread half over bacon, then season with salt and pepper. Spread cottage cheese. Sprinkle ¼ cup breadcrumbs around edge of dish to build up sides. Continue layering a third of tomato slices, onion to taste and a third of bacon. Spread remaining mayonnaise mixture over bacon. Sprinkle ¼ cup breadcrumbs around edge of dish and remaining breadcrumbs on top. Repeat layering with remaining tomato slices, onion to taste, remaining Cheddar and remaining bacon crumbles. Sprinkle with oregano and arrange bell pepper on top. Bake 45 minutes, then set aside 15 minutes before serving.

Restaurant Recipe

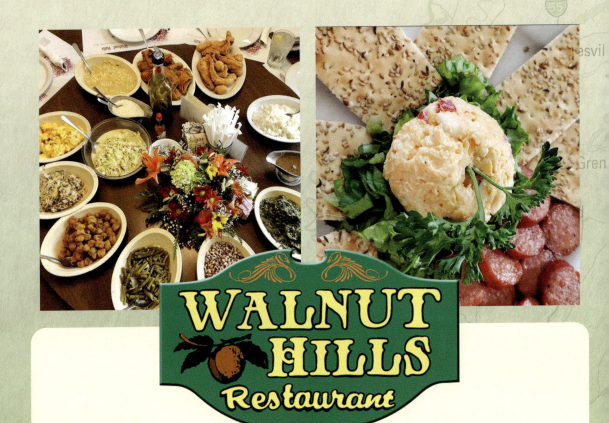

Walnut Hills Restaurant

1214 Adams Street
Vicksburg, MS 39183
601-638-4910
www.walnuthillsms.com
Find us on facebook

In 1980, Walnut Hills Restaurant opened as a round-table restaurant in the handsome old house on Adams Street. Part of the historic district, the house was built in 1880 by the Rogers family. Respecting tradition is what keeps the lunches and dinners popular at this Southern mecca. Joyce Clingan, owner, understands this and so does Miss Herdcine, a second-generation employee and chief cook at Walnut Hills for over thirty years. Herdcine's brother, Charles Williams; mother, Alma Robinson,; and son, Xavier, have also contributed to the restaurant's lengthy menu of Southern favorites. Come experience the traditions that make Walnut Hills one of the South's finest eateries.

Monday & Wednesday – Saturday: 11:00 am to 9:00 pm
Sunday: 11:00 am to 2:00 pm

Walnut Hills Bourbon Pie

For this recipe, Herdcine does not measure the bourbon, she just pours till it seems right.

Crust:

1 (16-ounce) box chocolate wafers, crushed, plus extra for garnish

¼ cup butter

Mix wafers and butter together. Press into 9-inch pie pan. (You may use a Keebler chocolate crust instead.)

Filling:

21 regular-size marshmallows, not miniature

1 cup evaporated milk

1 cup heavy cream

3 tablespoons bourbon or more to taste

In a saucepan over medium heat, heat marshmallows and milk, stirring constantly until marshmallows melt and mixture is smooth; be careful not to burn or boil. Set aside to cool. Whip cream until stiff peaks form. Add to cooled marshmallow mixture. Add bourbon and pour into pie crust. Refrigerate approximately 4 hours or until set. Top with whipped cream and chocolate crumbs.

Restaurant Recipe

COASTAL

Bay Saint Louis
Starfish Cafe 192

Biloxi
Gollotts Fresh Catch Seafood Restaurant 194
Mary Mahoney's Old French House 196
Petra Café 198
Slap Ya Momma's 200
Snapper's Seafood 202
Taranto's Crawfish 204
Tasty Tails Seafood House 206
White Pillars Restaurant & Lounge 208

Foxworth
Kane's Catfish, Seafood & Steakhouse 210

Gulfport
Murky Waters 212

Hattiesburg
Movie Star Restaurant 214
Murky Waters 212
Petra Café 198

Laurel
Hog Heaven Bar-B-Q 216
Pearl's Diner 218

Ocean Springs
Aunt Jenny's Catfish Restaurant 220
Murky Waters 212
The Shed Barbeque & Blues Joint 222
Vestige 224

Petal
Leatha's Bar-B-Que Inn 226

Richton
Fulmer's Farmstead & General Store 228

Seminary
Shady Acres Village 230

Waveland
Dat Kitchen Too 232

Waynesboro
The Dinner Bell Cafe 234

Wiggins
The Coffee Shop at Southern Turnings 236
Frosty Mug 238

211 Main Street
Bay Saint Louis, MS 39520
228-229-3503
www.starfishcafebsl.com
Find us on facebook

Starfish Café got its start in 2013 with the concept of providing job training and healthy food with open hearts. The café's commitment to wellness has been a cornerstone to providing healthy, locally grown food. Each plate or bowl is hand-crafted fresh when ordered. Offering unique menu items such as homemade gluten-free items, the goal is to provide a dining experience for those whose dietary needs may be outside a more traditional menu While most places give you a hefty tab Starfish Café is "pay what you want." Donations cover the cost of food and experience.

Thursday:
11:00 am to 7:00 pm
Friday & Saturday:
11:00 am to 8:00 pm

Beef Biscuit Roll

1 pound ground chuck
½ cup finely chopped onion
2 tablespoons finely chopped bell pepper
2 tablespoons mayonnaise
2 tablespoons ketchup
¾ teaspoon salt
⅛ teaspoon pepper
¼ teaspoon celery salt
1 egg, beaten
3¼ cups Bisquick mix
1 ⅔ cups milk, divided
1 (10.75-ounce) can cream of chicken soup

Preheat oven to 375°. In a bowl, combine chuck, onion, bell pepper, mayonnaise, ketchup, salt, pepper, celery salt and egg; mix well. In a 2-quart bowl, combine Bisquick and 1 cup milk with a fork to form a dough. Turn out on a lightly floured surface; roll or pat dough into a 12x15-inch rectangle. Spread beef mixture evenly over dough surface. Roll up like you would a jelly roll. Cut into 12 slices about 1½ inches thick. Place slices in a greased baking pan; bake 25 minutes. In a saucepan over medium heat combine soup and remaining milk; bring to a boil, stirring often. Pour over rolls as you serve them.

Local Favorite

Easy Chocolate Pie

1 (9-inch) unbaked pie crust
1 cup plus 3 tablespoons sugar, divided
2 tablespoons cocoa
3 tablespoons flour
2 eggs, separated
2 cups milk
1 tablespoon butter
1 teaspoon vanilla extract

Preheat oven to 400°. Using a fork, poke holes in bottom and sides of pie crust; bake 9 to 12 minutes. Remove from oven and set aside. In a saucepan, mix together 1 cup sugar, cocoa and flour. Add egg yolks and milk, stirring well. Add butter and vanilla and cook, stirring over medium heat until mixture thickens; pour in pie crust. Beat egg whites until stiff. Add remaining 3 tablespoons sugar and beat until fluffy. Top pie with meringue; bake until top is golden brown.

Local Favorite

200 East 8th Street
Biloxi, MS 39530
228-967-7448
Find us on facebook

You've no doubt heard the Gollott name associated with seafood. The Gollott seafood business began back in 1932, when Biloxi was known as the "Seafood Capital of the Country". Four generations later, Shawn Gollott started his own venture: Gollott's Fresh Catch. The restaurant opened in 2018 with the goal of making every customer who walks through the doors feel at home. Gollott does just that, serving up home-cooked meals and Southern hospitality. Many of the recipes are from Gollott's own mother, Trudy. Just look for her name on the menu "Our slogan is, 'your seafood, your neighbor, your backyard,'" said Shawn Gollott. "Giving people that welcoming feeling is our genuine intention, whether you are a local or a tourist. We pride ourselves on being authentic."

Sunday – Thursday: 11:00 am to 9:00 pm
Friday & Saturday: 11:00 am to 10:00 pm

Seafood Gumbo

2 tablespoons oil
2 tablespoons all-purpose flour
2 tablespoons bacon fat
3 cups diced okra
2 large onions, chopped
1 large sweet pepper, chopped
1 (14.5-ounce) can diced tomatoes
3 heads garlic, peeled and chopped (optional)
3 pounds wild-caught domestic shrimp, peeled
2 pounds wild-caught domestic crabmeat (or dressed crabs)
1 quart oysters, optional
Cayenne pepper to taste, optional
Salt to taste
Cooked white rice for serving

In a large stockpot, bring 2 quarts water to a slow boil. Meanwhile, heat oil in a skillet over medium heat; when hot, add flour, set to medium-low heat and stir constantly until a dark brown roux forms. Carefully stir 1 cup of the slow-boiling water into roux, then pour roux into the pot of slow-boiling water. In another skillet, heat bacon fat over medium heat; add okra and fry until slime is removed. Add onion and sweet pepper; cook until tender. Add tomatoes and garlic; cook 5 more minutes, then add vegetable mixture to the pot of slow-boiling water. Wash shrimp and pick through crabmeat for any remaining shell; add seafood to pot. Season to taste with cayenne and salt. Reduce heat to low and simmer for 1½ hours. Serve Seafood Gumbo hot over cooked rice.

Restaurant Recipe

110 Rue Magnolia
Biloxi, MS 39530
228-374-0163
www.marymahoneys.com
Find us on facebook

Mary Mahoney's Old French House is a Mississippi staple, serving visitors from all walks of life for more than fifty years. From presidents to celebrities to everyday people, millions have sat down for an upscale meal in this eighteenth-century home turned unique Southern eatery. Built in 1737 under the dominion of France, the Old French House features exposed brick walls, heart-pine floors, and open fireplaces. In 1962, Mary Mahoney, her husband, and her brother acquired the residence, and the rest is history. Today, visitors to Mary Mahoney's enjoy wonderful food and drink in a living monument to centuries past. Come experience the rich history and legendary cuisine of Mary Mahoney's.

Monday – Saturday: 11:00 am to 9:00 pm

Bread Pudding

6 slices day-old bread
1 teaspoon ground cinnamon
½ cup seedless raisins
2 tablespoons melted butter
4 eggs
¼ cup plus 2 tablespoons sugar
2 cups milk
1 teaspoon vanilla extract

Preheat oven to 350°. Tear bread into small pieces and place in a 1½-quart baking dish. Sprinkle bread with cinnamon, then toss with raisins and butter. Lightly toast in oven about 10 minutes; remove and set aside to cool. In a large bowl, mix eggs, sugar, milk and vanilla; pour into cooled bread mixture. Return to oven; bake 30 minutes or until solid.

Rum Sauce Topping:
2 cups milk
½ stick butter
½ cup sugar
2 tablespoons flour
1 tablespoon oil
1 tablespoon ground nutmeg
1 tablespoon vanilla extract
Rum to taste (or 1 teaspoon rum extract)

In a saucepan, add milk, butter and sugar; bring to a boil. In a bowl, mix together flour and oil to make a roux; add to boiling mixture to thicken, then remove from heat. Stir in nutmeg, vanilla and rum. Serve over warm Bread Pudding.

Restaurant Recipe

PETRA CAFE
GREEK & MEDITERRANEAN

6060 US Highway 49
Hattiesburg, MS 39401
601-268-8850

1680 Pass Road
Biloxi, MS 39531
228-280-8444

www.petracafe.net
Find us on facebook

Petra Café got its start in 2007 when owner, Ayman Al-Bataineh, decided to make Mississippi his home. Ayman found that the best way to capture the food and flavors he missed from his mother's cooking was to open his own restaurant. The café is named after the ancient city of Petra in Jordan which is considered the most famous and gorgeous site in the country. Petra offers delicious, authentic, fresh, home-cooked Greek and Mediterranean cuisine with Middle Eastern hospitality. Stop by and enjoy a relaxing atmosphere and sample for yourself the unique recipes that have been handed down for generations.

7 Days a Week:
11:00 am to 11:00 pm

Cauliflower with Tahini Sauce

1 cauliflower head, cut into florets
3 tablespoons olive oil
½ teaspoon cumin
½ teaspoon paprika
½ teaspoon rosemary
½ teaspoon turmeric
2 tablespoons butter
Pine nuts
Parsley
Pomegranate seeds
Tahini sauce

Preheat oven to 350°. In a large saucepan over high heat, bring 1 quart water to a boil. Drop florets into water; boil 5 to 7 minutes then drain. In a 9x13-inch casserole dish, mix florets with oil and spices. Roast in oven 30 minutes. Meanwhile, in a skillet over medium-low heat, melt butter and sauté pine nuts. Garnish cauliflower with pine nuts and remaining ingredients.

Family Favorite

Chicken Shawarma

Serve with garlic paste, onions, parsley and sumac pickles.

Boneless, skinless chicken breasts
1 large garlic clove, minced
2 tablespoons lemon juice
White pepper to taste
2 teaspoons salt
1 tablespoon ground cardamon
2 bay leaves
2 tablespoons olive oil
Tomato paste or puree

Butterfly chicken breasts and cut into strips. Mix garlic, lemon juice, pepper, salt, cardamom, bay leaves, olive oil and tomato paste in a zip-close bag. Add chicken strips and marinate at least 2 hours. Using a skillet over medium heat sauté strips to desired doneness.

Family Favorite

SLAP YA MOMMA'S BARBEQUE
BILOXI

1785 Beach Boulevard
Biloxi, MS 39531
228-456-0055
www.slapyamommas.com
Find us on facebook

Haul your butt to the beach for the best barbecue on the coast at Slap Ya Momma's. Their signature barbecue is smoked to perfection on-site. You will smell the pecan wood smoking that delicious meat as soon as you get there. Whether its ribs, brisket, pulled pork or chicken, this fall-off-the-bone barbecue is so good you will "wanna Slap Ya Momma" This fun destination restaurant specializes in whole chickens, smoked sausage, brisket, St. Louis ribs, and pulled pork by the pound. Family plates, barbeque specials, sandwiches, and appetizers available. Located right on the beach along Highway 90 in Biloxi, Slap Ya Momma's offer good barbecue, good drinks, and a good view. What more could you ask for?

Sunday – Thursday:
11:00 am to 9:00 pm
Friday & Saturday:
11:00 am to 10:00 pm

Smoked Jalapeño Poppers

Jalapeños
Brisket, pre-cooked
Cream cheese, softened
Bacon

Preheat smoker to 225°. Cut jalapeños in half lengthwise and remove seeds. Mix together brisket and cream cheese. Fill jalapeño cavities with brisket mixture. Wrap with bacon. Place in smoker for 1 hour. They are ready to eat. Once they cool, you can always place in oven at 350° for 10 minutes or fry in 350° oil for 3 to 4 minutes.

Family Recipe

Pork Belly Burnt Ends

Pork belly
Uncle Henry's dry rub (available in house or order by phone)
Slap Ya Momma's BBQ sauce

Heat smoker to 225°. Cut pork belly into equal square portions. Rub with dry rub. Place pork belly portions on a pan and smoke 2 hours. Remove pork belly from pan and place directly on the smoker for an additional hour. Remove meat from smoker, place in a deep pan and drizzle barbeque sauce over meat, to taste. Serve with additional sauce on side.

Family Recipe

Ultimate Nachos

Corn tortilla chips
Pulled pork
Rotel cheese sauce
Slap Ya Momma's BBQ Sauce (available in house or order by phone)
Baked beans
Coleslaw

Place chips on bottom of a large platter, top with rest of ingredients and enjoy.

Restaurant Recipe

Coastal

Snapper's Seafood

1699 Beach Boulevard
Biloxi, MS 39531
228-374-7962
snappersseafoodbiloxi.com
Find us on facebook

Snapper's Seafood is a local favorite and it's easy to see why. Their beachfront location offers gorgeous views of the beach from big windows in the dining room. Or sit on the outside deck and enjoy the refreshing ocean breeze. It's not just about the view, because Snapper's Seafood offers a delicious variety of fresh seafood that is guaranteed to please. Whether you are craving catfish po' boys or a seafood platter with shrimp, oysters, fish, and stuffed crabs or a delicious seafood salad, there is something for everyone. Be sure to check out their all-you-can-eat meals—including a delicious all-you-can-eat breakfast -- which will satisfy any appetite.

7 Days a Week:
8:00 am to 10:00 pm

Ham Hash

3 tablespoons oil
4 medium potatoes, finely chopped
2 medium carrots, finely chopped
½ small onion, finely chopped
1½ cups finely chopped cooked ham
Salt to taste

Heat oil in large skillet over medium heat. Fry potatoes, without stirring, until browned on bottom. Turn potatoes and cover with carrots, onion and ham. Cook another 8 minutes until potatoes are browned on bottom and tender. Add salt if needed.

Local Favorite

Homemade Chili

2 pounds ground beef
1 medium onion, chopped
1 green bell pepper, chopped
1 (12-ounce) can tomato paste
1 teaspoon salt
Freshly ground black pepper to taste
1 tablespoon packed brown sugar
½ teaspoon thyme
1 tablespoon cumin
2 tablespoons garlic powder
1 teaspoon cayenne pepper
1 teaspoon oregano
2 bay leaves
1 tablespoon barbecue sauce
2 tablespoons Worcestershire sauce
2 beef bouillon cubes
1 cup red wine

In a large saucepan oven over medium heat, sauté beef, onion and bell pepper, stirring often. When meat is browned, add remaining ingredients, along with 2 cups water; bring to a boil. Reduce to low heat and simmer several hours, stirring periodically and adding water as needed.

Local Favorite

Taranto's Crawfish

12404 John Lee Road
Biloxi, MS 39532
228-392-0990
Find us on facebook

Crawfish lovers, rejoice Taranto's Crawfish has everything you need to satisfy those mudbug cravings. Situated on the beautiful Gulf Coast, Taranto's Crawfish offers the Biloxi community and visitors perfectly seasoned crawfish, po' boys, and Southern-style seafood. Taranto's also offers a variety of rotating daily specials, appetizers, salads, sandwiches, steaks, fried platters, and home-style sides. With so many tasty options, you're sure to discover something wonderful. Visit Taranto's Crawfish and see why it's a Biloxi staple.

Tuesday – Saturday: 11:00 am to 9:00 pm

Bread Pudding

1½ loaves day-old bread
1½ cups raisins
1 cup white chocolate chips
1½ cups chopped pecans
1¼ quarts milk
2 cups sugar
2 tablespoons vanilla extract
1 tablespoon ground cinnamon
8 eggs
2 cups (4 sticks) melted butter

Preheat oven to 350°. Tear bread into pieces and place in a large baking dish. Sprinkle with raisins, white chocolate chips and pecans; toss. In a bowl, whisk together remaining ingredients; pour over bread. Bake 35 minutes or until golden brown and custard is set.

Restaurant Recipe

Coleslaw

½ cup sugar
½ cup buttermilk
½ cup mayonnaise
2½ tablespoons lemon juice
1½ tablespoons white vinegar
½ teaspoon salt
⅛ teaspoon black pepper
1 (10-ounce) package shredded cabbage
¼ cup shredded carrot

In a large bowl, whisk together sugar, buttermilk, mayonnaise, lemon juice, vinegar, salt and pepper. Add cabbage and carrot and toss to coat. Cover and chill before serving.

Restaurant Recipe

Tasty Tails Seafood House

188 Reynoir Street, Suite D
Biloxi, MS 39530
228-435-4140
Find us on facebook

Located in downtown Biloxi, Tasty Tails Seafood House is already one of the hottest dining destinations on the Mississippi Gulf Coast. With fresh crawfish, friendly service, and fantastic flavors, this seafood stop has become an instant classic. Enjoy the freshest seafood cooked to perfection, savor fried or boiled seafood choices with delicious side items, and make sure to try the signature Tasty Tail Sauce. Start your meal with the delicious homemade eggrolls or add some tasty gumbo to your meal. At Tasty Tails, there's something tasty for everyone

Sunday, Monday & Wednesday:
11:00 am to 9:00 pm
Thursday – Saturday:
11:00 am to midnight

Red Beans & Rice

The measurements might be a secret, but this recipe is quite easy to adapt to taste.

Vegetable oil
Andouille sausage, sliced into rounds
Sweet onion, diced
Celery, diced
Tomato paste
Garlic, minced
Salt-free Cajun seasoning to taste
Canned red beans, drained and rinsed
Chicken stock
Hot sauce to taste
1 bay leaf
Kosher salt and freshly ground black pepper to taste
Prepared rice for serving
Chopped fresh parsley for garnish

In a large stockpot over medium heat, heat vegetable oil. Sauté sausage until lightly browned; remove from pot and set aside. Add onion and celery; sauté 3 to 4 minutes or until tender. Stir in tomato paste, garlic and Cajun seasoning; cook 1 minute until garlic is fragrant. Stir in beans and several cups stock. Add hot sauce, bay leaf and sausage, then season to taste with salt and pepper. Bring to a boil; cover and simmer 15 minutes. Uncover and simmer 15 minutes or until liquid is reduced. Taste and adjust seasoning as needed. Serve with rice and a sprinkling of parsley.

Restaurant Recipe

Boiled Crawfish

Live crawfish
Garlic, minced
Granulated garlic
Seafood boil
Onions, halved

In a large tub, rinse crawfish well; pick through crawfish, removing any debris or dead crawfish. Repeat rinse as necessary until water runs clear. Fill a large stockpot one-third full with water; bring to a boil and add seasonings and onion to taste. Cover and cook 10 minutes. Transfer crawfish to pot, cover again and cook 3 minutes. Turn off heat and let sit, covered, 10 minutes. Enjoy.

Restaurant Recipe

White Pillars Restaurant & Lounge

1696 Beach Boulevard
Biloxi, MS 39531
228-207-0885
www.biloxiwhitepillars.com
Find us on facebook

White Pillars Restaurant & Lounge is a farm-to-table restaurant located on the Mississippi Gulf Coast in a restored and beautifully updated 1900-era beachfront home. Home to a restaurant once before, the house found new life in 2017 when Chef Austin Sumrall and his wife, Tresse, opened it under the White Pillars moniker. The Sumralls are passionate about showcasing the wonderful things the coast and the state of Mississippi have to offer. The restaurant uses locally sourced farm-fresh ingredients to compose a menu that changes daily according to ingredient availability and the changing seasons. White Pillars offers craft cocktails, local beers, wine, and a dining experience that is second to none.

Wednesday – Saturday: 11:30 am to 9:00 pm
BRUNCH:
Sunday: 10:00 am to 2:00 pm
WP LOUNGE:
Tuesday: 4:00 am to 9:00 pm

Oyster Hand Pies

1 cup each small-diced celery, onion and green bell pepper

1 tablespoon minced garlic

½ tablespoon chopped thyme

2 tablespoons olive oil

1 pint rough-chopped oysters, liquor reserved

1 pound ground beef

1 tablespoon hot sauce

2 tablespoons Worcestershire sauce

1 to 2 cups dried breadcrumbs

½ cup chopped fresh parsley

½ cup chopped green onions

Salt and pepper to taste

Premade hand-pie crusts, raw

In a saucepan, sweat vegetables and thyme in oil until tender. Add oysters and beef; brown beef. Stir in oyster liquor, hot sauce and Worcestershire. Add remaining ingredients except pie crust, adjusting breadcrumbs as needed for desired consistency. Fill crusts with filling and crimp closed. Bake at 375° or fry at 350° until golden brown.

Rémoulade:

3 cups basic aioli

1 cup coarse mustard

1 lemon, juiced

1 tablespoon hot sauce

2 tablespoons chopped capers

3 eggs, hard-boiled and grated

2 tablespoons chopped chives

Salt and pepper to taste

In a bowl, mix all ingredients. Serve hand pies with rémoulade.

Restaurant Recipe

Smokehouse Gumbo

2 cups peanut oil

2½ cups all-purpose flour

6 large yellow onions, diced small

6 red bell peppers, diced small

3 bunches celery, diced small

½ head garlic, minced

1 bottle light beer

14 cups chicken stock

Salt and pepper

4 whole chickens, roasted with salt, pepper and thyme

1 quart braised collards

1 pound smoked sausage, sliced and sautéed

Prepared rice for serving

Green onions, sliced on a bias

In a large stockpot over low heat, make a dark roux with oil and flour, taking care not to burn flour. Add onion, bell pepper, celery and garlic, then deglaze with beer. Add stock, salt and pepper. Add chicken, collards and sausage; cover and simmer 30 minutes. Remove lid and simmer 30 minutes more. Serve over rice and garnish with green onion.

Restaurant Recipe

Kane's Catfish, Seafood & Steakhouse

3129 Highway 35 South
Foxworth, MS 39483
601-731-9626
Find us on facebook

Wayne and Bobbie Regan opened Kane's in the little town of Foxworth in October 2005. They pride themselves on family and generosity for their community. The menu features a variety of foods such as Angus beef steaks, seafood, and Mississippi farm-raised catfish which is fresh weekly. Kane's has an active catering business and they open their doors on off days to help with local fundraisers such as the Cystic Fibrosis Foundation, churches, baseball teams, Relay for Life, and many others. When you leave Kane's, you leave as a family member.

Thursday – Saturday:
4:00 pm to 9:00 pm

Bourbon Balls

3 cups crushed vanilla wafers
3 tablespoons white corn syrup
1 cup powdered sugar
½ cup cocoa
1 cup chopped pecans
½ cup bourbon

In a bowl, mix all ingredients together and form into small balls. Roll balls in your choice of covering: powdered sugar, cocoa, melted chocolate, nuts or coconut. They are all good.

Local Favorite

Enchilada Casserole

1 pound ground beef
½ cup finely chopped onion
1 teaspoon garlic powder
½ teaspoon cumin
1 (10-ounce) can mild enchilada sauce
1 (12-ounce) package corn tortillas
1 cup shredded Cheddar cheese
1 cup shredded Monterey Jack cheese

Preheat oven to 325°. In a skillet over medium heat, brown meat until crumbly; drain. Add onion, garlic powder, cumin, enchilada sauce and half an enchilada sauce can of water. Simmer 15 minutes, stirring occasionally. Layer tortillas, meat sauce and cheeses in 2 layers in a greased 9x13-inch baking dish. Bake 15 minutes or until brown and bubbly.

Local Favorite

Coastal

Murky Waters
Blues n BBQ

Gulfport Location:
1320 27th Avenue
Gulfport, MS 39501
228-214-4420

Hattiesburg Location:
1605 Hardy Street
Hattiesburg, MS 39401
601-336-8529

Ocean Springs Location:
1212 Government Street
Ocean Springs, MS 39564
228-215-1114

www.murkywatersbbq.com
Find us on facebook

With award-winning barbecue, local craft brews, and authentic live blues, you'll discover a true Mississippi hangout at any of Murky Waters' three locations. Enjoy six nights of music from Ocean Springs' Sunday Open Blues Jam to listening to your favorite local musician during Wing Night Wednesday in Gulfport or Hattiesburg. From Grammy-winning artists to regional breakthroughs, Murky Waters hosts some of the South's most talented musicians. Enjoy the music but come for the dry-rubbed barbecue, slow smoked with local pecan wood. Locally owned and operated, Murky Waters is a fabulous barbecue restaurant and blues club not to be missed.

Sunday – Tuesday: 11:00 am to 9:00 pm
Wednesday & Thursday: 11:00 am to 10:00 pm
Friday: 11:00 am to 11:00 pm
Saturday: 11:00 am to midnight

Reuben Casserole

1 (12-ounce) can corned beef
1 (16-ounce) can sauerkraut, drained
2 cups shredded Swiss cheese
½ cup Thousand Island dressing
1 large tomato, sliced
1 cup pumpernickel breadcrumbs
2 tablespoons margarine
Salt and pepper to taste
2 tablespoons caraway seeds

Preheat oven to 350°. Using a 2-quart lightly greased casserole dish, layer each ingredient in order, staring with corned beef and ending with caraway seeds. Bake 30 minutes. Rest 5 minutes before serving.

Local Favorite

Kum Back Sauce

1 teaspoon mustard
2 garlic cloves, minced
Dash Tabasco sauce
1 lemon, juiced
2 cups mayonnaise
1 tablespoon Worcestershire sauce
Dash paprika
1 (12-ounce) bottle chili sauce
1 teaspoon pepper
2 tablespoons grated onion

Mix all ingredients in blender until smooth. Chill until ready to use.

Local Favorite

5209 Old Highway 11
Hattiesburg, MS 39402
601-264-0606
www.moviestarrestaurant.com
Find us on facebook

Originally opened in the old Movie Star lingerie factory building from where it gets its name, Movie Star Restaurant is a Hattiesburg mainstay. At Movie Star Restaurant, the emphasis is on the classics, so it's the place to go if you're looking for fried chicken like your momma used to make and good old-fashioned Southern hospitality. With an atmosphere set by collections of antiques on display, you get to experience an old-timey feel when you dine in. Famous for its home-style buffet, Movie Star serves up dozens of Southern classics, from turnip greens to fried pork chops. Movie Star Restaurant has it all and country-fried charm to boot.

Sunday – Friday: 11:00 am to 2:00 pm
Friday & Saturday: 5:00 pm to 8:00 pm

Green Bean Almondine

2 (14.5-ounce) cans cut green beans (we prefer Del Monte)

1 chicken bouillon cube

¼ teaspoon garlic powder

2 tablespoons butter

¼ cup slivered almonds

¼ teaspoon garlic salt

In a saucepan over medium heat, bring green beans with chicken bouillon and garlic powder to a boil. Reduce heat and simmer 20 minutes. While beans cook, melt butter in skillet over medium heat, add almonds and garlic salt stirring constantly for 5 minutes or until toasted lightly brown, but not burned. Drain beans; pour into shallow serving bowl. Pour almonds and butter drippings in center. Serve.

Family Favorite

Killer Chicken

2 (14.5-ounce) cans cut green beans, drained

Garlic powder to taste

2 large potatoes, peeled and cubed

1 small bag baby carrots, cut in half

Lawry's seasoning salt to taste

1 whole chicken, cut up

Preheat oven to 375°. Using an 11x17-inch sheet pan, cover a third with green beans seasoned with garlic powder, another third with potatoes and remaining third with carrots both seasoned with Lawry's. Bake 30 to 45 minutes. Heavily season chicken with Lawry's. Remove foil and completely cover vegetables with chicken, skin side up. Bake 1 hour covered or until potatoes and carrots are tender and chicken has an internal temperature of 165°.

Family Favorite

Hog Heaven Bar-B-Q

3204 Ellisville Boulevard
Laurel, MS 39440
601-426-9795
www.hogheavenbbqlaurel.com
Find us on facebook

"Good barbecue, good folks, and good times." That's what Hog Heaven Bar-B-Q is all about. Since 2004, this husband-and-wife team has been sharing delicious barbecue and Southern comfort food favorites with the Laurel community. It's a relaxed, easygoing place, but they're serious about the food they serve. You'll taste the hard work in every meal you enjoy with them. Whether you're craving baby back ribs, drumettes, or a plate piled high with their homemade meatloaf and a side of cobbler, Hog Heaven Bar-B-Q will always have your fix. And they'll serve it up with a smile and a side of Southern hospitality

Monday – Thursday: 10:00 am to 3:00 pm
Friday & Saturday: 10:00 am to 8:00 pm
Sunday: 11:00 am to 2:00 pm

Deviled Eggs

6 eggs, hard-boiled

¼ cup mayonnaise

1 to 2 tablespoons prepared horseradish

½ teaspoon dill weed

¼ teaspoon ground mustard

⅛ teaspoon salt

Dash pepper

Paprika

Cut eggs in half lengthwise. Remove yolks; set whites aside. In a bowl, mash yolks; add mayonnaise, horseradish, dill, mustard, salt and pepper. Mix well. Pipe or spoon into egg whites. Sprinkle with paprika. Refrigerate before serving.

Local Favorite

Herbed Rice

1 onion, finely chopped

3 tablespoons melted butter

1 cup uncooked rice

3 cups chicken broth

¾ teaspoon basil

¾ teaspoon marjoram

½ teaspoon sage

¼ teaspoon thyme

¼ teaspoon curry powder

In a medium saucepan, sauté onion in butter until translucent. Add rice; cook 2 minutes, stirring. Add remaining ingredients; bring to a boil and cover. Reduce heat to low and cook 30 minutes or until all broth is absorbed and rice is cooked through.

Local Favorite

THE JEWEL OF THE CRESCENT LINE

PEARL'S DINER
LAUREL · MISS.
EST · 2017

330 Magnolia Street
Laurel, MS 39440
601-682-0945
mspearlsworld.com
Find us on facebook

Pearl's Diner is a family-style restaurant that opened its doors in 2017. Ms. Pearl serves up true classic Southern food with blue plate lunches that consist of one meat, your choice of two or three sides, and cornbread. The meat choices vary from day to day but her fried chicken is a staple and a must try. Don't forget the mac and cheese, greens, and black-eyed peas, they are just as delicious. Great home-cooked food isn't all Pearl's is known for. Customers consistently rave about the employees and Ms. Pearl's true Southern hospitality.

Monday – Saturday: 11:00 am to 2:00 pm

Ms. Pearl's Chicken Spaghetti

- 1 (12-ounce) package spaghetti
- 1 (10-ounce) can diced tomatoes
- ½ each green, yellow and red bell pepper, chopped
- 2 cups chicken broth
- 2½ cups cooked, chopped chicken breast
- 1 (10.75-ounce) can condensed cream of mushroom soup
- ½ (10.75-ounce) can condensed cream of chicken soup
- Salt and pepper to taste
- 1 (8-ounce) block sharp Cheddar cheese, shredded

Preheat oven to 350°. Bring a large pot of lightly salted water to a boil. Add pasta and cook for 8 to 10 minutes or until al dente; drain and return to pot. To the pasta, add tomatoes, bell peppers, broth, chicken, soups, salt and pepper. Mix well. Pour into an 11x13-inch casserole dish. Top with cheese. Bake uncovered 15 to 20 minutes or until cheese is melted. Enjoy.

Family Favorite

Ms. Pearl's Pot Roast with Potatoes & Carrots

- 2 tablespoons olive oil or vegetable oil
- 2-to-3 pound chuck roast
- 1 teaspoon Tony Chachere's Creole Seasoning
- 1 teaspoon Accent, optional
- ½ teaspoon black pepper
- 1 (2-ounce) box Lipton onion soup mix
- ½ yellow onion, sliced
- 4 cups beef broth, plus more if needed
- 1 (10.75-ounce) can condensed cream of mushroom soup
- 3 to 4 large carrots, peeled and sliced into 1-inch pieces
- 3 to 4 large russet potatoes, peeled and sliced into 1-inch wedges

Preheat oven to 375°. Place a large cast-iron pot over high heat; add oil. Season roast on both sides and sear. Add onion as you sear. Add broth and soup making sure to cover roast at least halfway up sides. Cover and bake 1½ hours. Check liquid in pot and add another cup or so, if needed. Reduce heat to 350°; bake 1 hour. Remove lid, add carrots and potatoes; bake uncovered 45 minutes longer or until roast is tender and vegetable are fork-tender.

Family Favorite

Aunt Jenny's Catfish Restaurant

1217 Washington Avenue
Ocean Springs, MS 39564
228-875-9201
www.auntjennyscatfish.com
Find us on facebook

Aunt Jenny's Catfish Restaurant is family-owned and family-operated in a historic antebellum home built in the 1800s. The restaurant offers a spectacular view of 500-year-old oak trees and the peaceful waters of historic Fort Bayou. While enjoying the beautiful scenery, you can dine on hand-fed catfish fillets, Southern fried chicken, and golden fried shrimp. After dinner, head downstairs to the Julep Room and listen to live music in the hangout spot of "the King of Rock and Roll" Elvis Presley. On your way out, don't forget to stop by the Chickadee Nest gift shop in the lobby offering handmade pottery made by local artists.

Monday – Wednesday: 4:00 pm to 9:00 pm
Thursday: 11:00 am to 9:00 pm
Friday & Saturday: 11:00 am to 9:30 pm
Sunday: 11:00 am to 8:00 pm

Braised Mushrooms

2 pounds fresh button mushrooms
¼ cup reduced-sodium soy sauce
¼ cup low-sodium beef broth
¼ cup honey
2 tablespoons dry sherry
2 tablespoons rice vinegar
3 garlic cloves, minced
1 teaspoon grated fresh ginger
2 green onions, finely chopped
2 tablespoons butter

Place mushrooms in a 4-quart slow cooker. In a small bowl, stir together soy sauce, broth, honey, sherry, vinegar, garlic and ginger; pour over mushrooms. Cover and cook on low 8 to 10 hours or on high 4 to 5 hours. Stir in green onions and butter. Serve as an appetizer or over hot cooked rice.

Local Favorite

Red Rice

14 slices bacon
2 large red bell peppers, chopped
1 medium onion, chopped
4 teaspoons dried thyme
1 cup tomato paste
3 cups uncooked long-grain rice
6 cups chicken broth
1 tablespoon Tabasco sauce

In a large skillet over medium heat, fry bacon until crisp; remove from skillet, drain on paper towels and crumble. Leave 3 tablespoons bacon drippings in skillet. Add peppers, onion and thyme; sauté 5 minutes. Mix in bacon, tomato paste, rice, broth and Tabasco. Reduce heat, cover and simmer 30 minutes or until rice is tender.

Local Favorite

THE SHED
BARBEQUE & BLUES JOINT

7501 Highway 57
Ocean Springs, MS 39565
228-875-9590
www.theshedbbq.com
Find us on facebook

Welcome to The Shed Barbeque & Blues Joint, home of award-winning barbecue and the blues. Serving the Ocean Springs community since 2001, The Shed is not a fancy restaurant. In fact, it's not really a restaurant at all. It's a full-fledged joint. The Shed is an experience, a destination to enjoy. ShedHeds bring their families, sit around the bonfires, eat the fantastic barbecue, and listen to live music every weekend. Come join the party and don't forget to purchase some of their famous barbeque sauce.

Sunday – Thursday: 8:00 am to 9:00 pm
Friday & Saturday: 8:00 am to 10:00 pm

Brad's Award-Winning Slow-Smoked Brisket

1½ cups garlic salt
¾ cup fresh ground black pepper
15 cups turbinado sugar
1½ cups paprika
½ cup chili powder
¾ cup ground cumin
¼ cup dried oregano
12 to 16 pounds brisket

In a bowl, whisk together seasonings and herb; rub in and fully cover brisket with seasoning mixture. Refrigerate brisket at least 30 minutes to allow rub to penetrate. Using pecan wood, heat smoker to 260°. Remove brisket from refrigerator and place in smoker. Smoke 10 to 12 hours or until brisket reaches internal temperature of 190° to 195°. Serve with The Shed BBQ sauce.

Restaurant Recipe

Southern Dry Rub

GREAT on Chicken, Pork, and Beef.

¼ cup white pepper
2 cups paprika
1 cup cumin
2 cups garlic salt
1 cup (coarse-ground) black pepper
½ cup chili powder
¼ cup dried oregano
8 cups dark brown sugar

Mix spices well before adding sugar. This will ensure your spices are evenly distributed.

Restaurant Recipe

Vestige

715 Washington Avenue
Ocean Springs, MS 39564
228-818-9699
www.vestigerestaurant.com
Find us on facebook

Vestige is a contemporary American restaurant in beautiful, historic downtown Ocean Springs. The restaurant is locally owned by Ocean Springs native and chef Alex Perry and his wife, Kumi Omori. The fare is often inspired by flavors and techniques of Japan, where Kumi grew up. Alex finds it intriguing and delicious. When they serve Southern staples or freshly baked bread, it's usually Kumi behind the cooking. She finds them fascinating as a transplant to the beautiful Gulf Coast. Alex and Kumi believe in seasonality, sustainability, and locality whenever possible. These tenets allow them to create wholesome dishes that they feel good about serving and eating.

Tuesday – Saturday: 5:30 pm to 9:00 pm

Best-Ever Pecan Pie

3 eggs, slightly beaten
1 cup dark corn syrup
1 cup sugar
2 tablespoons butter
1 teaspoon vanilla extract
1½ cups pecans
1 (9-inch) unbaked pie crust

Preheat oven to 350°. In a large bowl, mix all ingredients except pecans and pie crust until well blended. Stir in pecans; pour mixture into pie crust. Bake 50 to 55 minutes or until knife inserted in center comes out clean. Cool and serve.

Local Favorite

Liver and Onions

2 tablespoons vegetable oil
⅔ pound beef or pork liver, sliced
4 tablespoons flour
¾ teaspoon salt
Pepper to taste
1 large onion, sliced

Heat oil in frying pan over medium heat. Coat liver with flour; place in pan, brown on 1 side and flip. Sprinkle with salt and pepper; place onion on top. Add 3 tablespoons water; turn heat to low and cover tightly. Cook 20 minutes or until tender, occasionally adding water as needed.

Local Favorite

Leatha's Bar-B-Que Inn

1225 MS Highway 42
Petal, MS 39465
769-390-7819
Find us on facebook

Since the 1970s, Leatha's Bar-B-Que Inn has been serving up delicious barbecue in a humble setting. Originally opened in Foxworth, Leatha Jackson moved the business to Hattiesburg in 2000. Now it is located in Petal. Leatha passed in 2013, but her family continues to honor her memory by carrying on her legacy and serving Leatha's famous barbecue. Guests will enjoy tender ribs that fall off the bone, slow-cooked pulled pork, smoked sausage, smoked chicken, and homemade sides. Don't forget dessert. From pecan pie to strawberry cheesecake to Bonnie's toffee pie, Leatha's has it all.

Tuesday – Saturday: 11:00 am to 9:00 pm

Smoked Salmon Fillets

2 cups Leatha's lemon pepper (or BBQ) seasoning

1 cup peanut oil plus more for brushing

8 to 10 salmon fillets, raw

Preheat smoker to 350°. In a bowl, mix together seasoning and oil to make a wet rub; lightly brush over salmon. Place salmon in smoker on a sheet of foil brushed with peanut oil to prevent sticking. Cook 8 to 10 minutes or until internal temperature is 145°. Fillets should be light pink when done.

Restaurant Recipe

Smoked Turkey Legs

2 cups Leatha's BBQ seasoning

1 cup peanut oil

7 turkey legs, raw

Preheat smoker to 350°. In a bowl, mix together seasoning and oil to make a wet rub; lightly brush rub over turkey legs. Place turkey legs in smoker 1½ to 2 hours, rotating as needed to achieve even golden brown color. Remove turkey legs and wrap individually with foil; return to smoker 1 hour or until internal temperature reaches 165°.

Restaurant Recipe

Fulmer's Farmstead
& GENERAL STORE

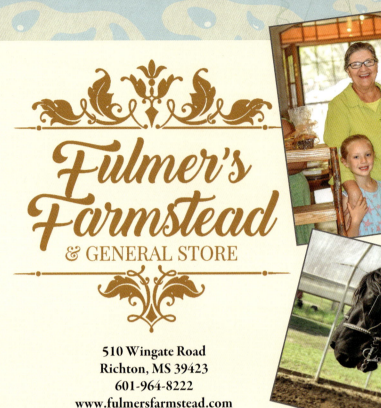

510 Wingate Road
Richton, MS 39423
601-964-8222
www.fulmersfarmstead.com
Find us on facebook

Fulmer's Farmstead and General Store offers a bakery, deli, delicious hot plate lunches, and so much more. It is the perfect destination for all your homestead needs with a full line of bulk foods, homemade jams and jellies, in-season produce, and an outstanding assortment of horsedrawn equipment. Produce comes right off the family's horsedrawn farm where the farm work is done with draft horses. Come for a great meal, shop for some unique gifts, and take home fresh baked bread and pies. Fulmer's General Store is a unique experience you won't want to miss.

Monday – Saturday: 8:00 am to 5:00 pm

Vidalia Onion Casserole

6 onions, sliced
1 stick butter
1 cup cooked rice
1 (8-ounce) carton whipping cream
4 ounces shredded cheese, plus extra for topping
Paprika

Preheat oven to 350°. In a skillet over medium heat, sauté onions in butter. Add rice, whipping cream and cheese, mix together. Pour into baking dish. Sprinkle extra cheese on top, then paprika. Bake 30 minutes.

Restaurant Recipe

Eggplant Casserole

2 to 3 pounds eggplant, cut into 2-inch cubes
5 strips bacon
1 large onion, diced
40 saltine crackers, crushed
1 large egg, beaten
½ cup evaporated milk, plus extra if needed
Salt and pepper to taste
1 cup grated Cheddar cheese

Preheat oven to 400°. Place eggplant into a large saucepan over medium heat and cover with salted water. Bring to a boil; reduce heat to simmer and cook until tender. Drain and set aside. Chop bacon and sauté in skillet until half done. Add onion; cook until lightly browned. In a large mixing bowl, combine eggplant, bacon, onion and drippings. Add crackers. Stir in egg, milk and seasoning. If mixture appears stiff, add more milk. Pour into a 2-quart casserole dish. Sprinkle with cheese. Cover and bake 15 to 20 minutes or until bubbly. Let rest before serving.

Restaurant Recipe

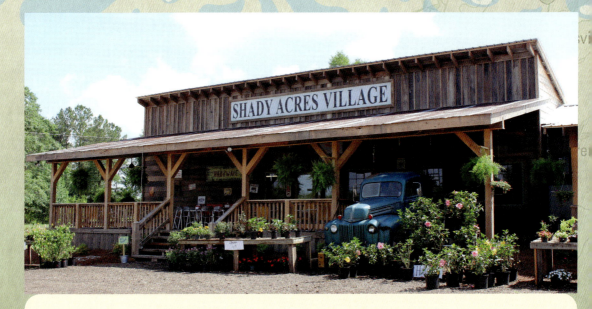

Shady Acres Village

624 Highway 49
Seminary, MS 39479
601-722-4114
www.shadyacresvillage.com
Find us on facebook

Shady Acres Village is a family-style restaurant featuring daily blue plate specials, plus a general store with fresh produce, homemade jams, jellies, candies, cookies, and homemade cakes and pies baked on-site. Shady Acres is also a unique gift shop featuring Mississippi pottery, T-shirts and home decor. Come hungry and enjoy Southern-style cooking like fried green tomatoes, homemade chicken salad, and Mississippi-grown sweet potato fries, or choose scrumptious barbecue ribs or chicken, and so much more. Whatever you're in the mood for, you can find it at Shady Acres Village.

CAFE:
Monday – Saturday: 10:30 am to 4:00 pm
GENERAL STORE:
Monday – Saturday: 9:00 am to 5:00 pm

Cheesy Potato Soup

3 pounds red potatoes, diced into ½-inch cubes

¼ cup margarine

¼ cup flour

8 cups half-and-half

1 (1-pound) package Velveeta cheese, melted

White pepper to taste

Garlic powder to taste

1 teaspoon hot pepper sauce

½ pound bacon, fried crispy, crumbled

1 cup shredded Cheddar cheese

½ cup chopped fresh chives

½ cup chopped fresh parsley

Add potatoes to a large stockpot, cover with water and boil until three-quarters of the way cooked. In another large saucepan over low heat, melt margarine and stir in flour, mixing until smooth. Add half-and-half, stirring constantly, until smooth and thickened. Add Velveeta and mix well. Drain potatoes; add to cheese mixture. Stir in pepper, garlic powder and hot sauce; cook another 30 minutes, stirring occasionally. Garnish each bowl with crumbled bacon, shredded cheese, chives and parsley on top.

Family Favorite

Hash Brown Casserole

1 (28-ounce) package Southern style hash browns

1 (8-ounce) package shredded Cheddar cheese

1 (10.75 ounce) can cream of chicken soup

1 stick butter

1 small onion, diced

Salt and pepper to taste

Preheat oven to 350°. Combine all ingredients and pour into a greased 9x13-inch casserole dish. Bake 50 to 60 minutes.

Family Favorite

Cream Cheese Chili

2 (16-ounce) cans chili beans, drained

2 (15-ounce) cans corn

2 (10-ounce) cans Rotel tomatoes

3 (12.5-ounce) cans chicken

2 (1-ounce) packages ranch dressing mix

2 teaspoons cumin

2 teaspoons onion powder

2 teaspoons chili powder

2 (8-ounce) packages cream cheese, softened

Put all ingredients into slow cooker. Stir to mix well. Turn setting to low and cook 8 hours.

Family Favorite

Dat Kitchen Too

714 Highway 90
Waveland, MS 39576
228-467-7242
Find us on facebook

Dat Kitchen Too is a family-style restaurant located in the town of Waveland. It is considered a hidden gem in the restaurant world with hand-painted murals that adorn the walls. Their menu is quite extensive and features anything you could possibly imagine from po' boys, seafood, soups, salads, pasta dishes, Southern-style dishes, Cajun dishes and daily blue plate specials. But if you ask owner, Hugh, he will tell you that the best dish in the house is Catfish Katrina. Next time you are in town don't forget to stop at Dat Kitchen Too.

Monday – Thursday:
7:00 am to 8:30 pm
Friday & Saturday:
7:00 am to 9:00 pm
Sunday:
7:00 am to 3:00 pm

Meatloaf

15 pounds ground beef
1½ cups diced onions
1½ cups diced bell pepper
1 cup granulated garlic
1½ (2-ounce) boxes onion soup mix
⅓ cup Italian seasoning
1 cup Worcestershire sauce
½ cup Tony Chachere's Original Creole seasoning
10 eggs, beaten
1 cup breadcrumbs

Preheat oven to 350°. Mix all ingredients together. Form into loaf. Bake 2 to 2½ hours. Best when served with mashed potatoes and vegetables.

Restaurant Recipe

BBQ Shrimp

16 to 20 count shrimp, as many as will fill pan
Extra virgin olive oil
Black pepper to taste
Cayenne pepper to taste
Tony Chachere's Original Creole seasoning to taste
Garlic powder to taste
Liquid crab boil to taste
Fresh garlic cloves, minced
Worcestershire sauce to taste
2 lemons, thinly sliced
2 sticks margarine
Parsley flakes

Preheat oven to 400°. Layer shrimp across the bottom of and aluminum pan (do not stack). Drizzle olive oil over shrimp. Sprinkle with black pepper, cayenne pepper, Tony's seasoning, garlic powder, liquid crab boil, fresh garlic and Worcestershire. Place sliced lemons evenly on top; slice butter into pats and place on top. Sprinkle parsley flakes over top. Cover with foil and bake 30 minutes.

Family Favorite

The Dinner Bell Café

601 Mississippi Drive
Waynesboro, MS 39367
601-735-0480
Find us on facebook

The Dinner Bell Café is a family-style restaurant owned by Todd and Louise Wise. The restaurant features a daily buffet where you can find anything from Mississippi-raised catfish baked or fried, greens, mac and cheese, and cornbread. They also have a full salad bar that is offered daily. Save room for dessert because they offer up an assortment of sweet treats to choose from, including homemade peach cobbler. When you want a good hearty meal, make your way to The Dinner Bell Café where you will always leave satisfied.

Monday – Friday:
8:00 am to 2:00 pm
Sunday:
10:30 am to 2:00 pm

Sweet Potato Casserole

3 cups cooked and mashed sweet potatoes
1½ cups sugar
½ cup melted butter or margarine
2 eggs, well beaten
1 teaspoon vanilla
⅓ cup Pet Milk

Preheat oven to 350°. In a medium bowl, combine all ingredients; pour into an 8-inch square casserole dish. Add topping.

Topping:

½ cup packed brown sugar
¼ cup flour
2½ tablespoons melted butter or margarine
½ to 1 cup chopped pecans.

In a small bowl, mix sugar, flour and butter; crumble evenly over top of casserole. Sprinkle with pecans. Bake for 30 to 40 minutes until heated through.

Restaurant Recipe

Citrus Cooler

2½ cups sugar

1 (46-ounce) can pineapple juice

1 (46-ounce) can orange juice (Donald Duck red can)

1½ cups lemon juice (Minute Maid frozen)

1½ cups ginger ale, chilled

In a saucepan over medium heat, bring 2½ cups water and sugar to a boil. Cook until sugar dissolves. Pour into a 4½-quart freezer-safe container. Stir in all juices and freeze. Remove from freezer several hours before serving; stir in ginger ale. Mixture should be slushy.

Restaurant Recipe

Doritos Casserole

1 (16-ounce) bag Doritos chips, crushed and divided

1 pound ground chuck

1 (8-ounce) package shredded medium Cheddar cheese

1 (8-ounce) carton sour cream

1 (10-ounce) can diced Rotel tomatoes

1 (10.75-ounce) can cream of chicken soup

1 (10.75-ounce) can cream of mushroom soup

Preheat oven to 400°. Place half of Doritos in bottom of a 9x13-inch casserole dish. Brown meat and drain. Top chips with meat and cheese. In a medium bowl, mix sour cream, tomatoes and soups together; pour over cheese. Sprinkle with remaining chips. Bake 30 minutes until hot and bubbly.

Restaurant Recipe

THE COFFEE SHOP AT Southern TURNINGS

145 East Pine Avenue
Wiggins, MS 39577
601-523-1991
www.southernturnings.com
Find us on facebook

Located on a brick street in the original downtown section of Wiggins, the store is a creative mix of a wood-turning studio, coffee shop, gift store, and art gallery. A welcoming atmosphere is encompassed in a 100-year-old brick building that provides the visitor with an experience like no other. Sit and enjoy warm conversation, while sipping on a Mississippi-roasted gourmet coffee and dining on a delicious locally baked pastry. The next time you find yourself on Highway 49 between Gulfport and Hattiesburg, make sure you plan a destination stop in downtown Wiggins.

Monday – Friday:
7:30 am to 5:30 pm
Saturday:
9:00 am to 5:00 pm

Crème Brûlée Latte

½ ounce Torani caramel sauce plus more to drizzle on top

½ ounce Torani French vanilla syrup

1 ounce espresso (or strong coffee)

6 ounces steamed milk

Whipped cream

Stir together caramel sauce, vanilla syrup, coffee and milk. Top with whipped cream and caramel drizzle.

Restaurant Recipe

The Glass Slipper

⅓ ounce Torani white chocolate syrup plus more to drizzle on top

⅓ ounce Torani pumpkin spice syrup

1 ounce espresso or (strong coffee)

6 ounces steamed milk

Whipped cream

Cinnamon sugar

Blue sprinkles

Stir together chocolate syrup, pumpkin spice syrup, espresso and milk. Top with whipped cream, white chocolate drizzle, cinnamon sugar and blue sprinkles.

Restaurant Recipe

Kat's Company Chicken

This dish came from my Aunt Katherine, it's our all-time favorite chicken recipe.

10 to 12 chicken tenderloins

5 to 6 slices bacon, cut in half

1 (8-ounce) carton sour cream

1 (10.75-ounce) can cream of mushroom soup

1 (10.75-ounce) can cream of chicken soup

1 tablespoon Worcestershire sauce

½ teaspoon garlic salt

½ teaspoon celery salt

1 teaspoon dried parsley

Turn oven on to broil. Arrange tenderloins in a 9x13-inch casserole dish. Cover each piece completely with bacon strip. Place under broiler until bacon begins to brown, about 3 minutes. Turn oven down to 325°. In a large bowl, mix together remaining ingredients. Cover chicken with soup mixture. Cover dish with foil and bake 90 minutes. Remove foil and continue to bake another 30 minutes. Serve over rice.

Family favorite

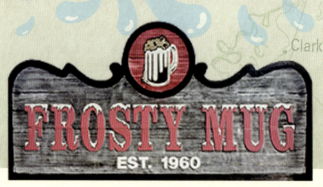

514 Magnolia Drive South
Wiggins, MS 39577
www.frostymugwiggins.com
Find us on facebook

Frosty Mug has been a Wiggins tradition for more than sixty years. Famous for the Lot O Burger, the restaurant also has a wide selection of food items, from po' boys and sandwiches to wraps and salads. Frosty Mug also offers shakes, storms, sundaes, snow cones, and other tasty sweet treats. In addition to good food, you can't beat the quality service. Come enjoy something delicious on the open patio with friends and family.

Monday – Saturday:
10:00 am to 8:00 pm

Sea Foam

1½ cups light brown sugar
½ cup white sugar
½ cup hot water
¼ cup light corn syrup
¼ teaspoon salt
2 egg whites
1 teaspoon vanilla extract
½ cup chopped pecans, optional

In a buttered 1½-quart saucepan, combine sugars, water, corn syrup, and salt; set over medium heat and cook, stirring constantly, until sugars dissolve and mixture comes to a boil. Stop stirring and continue cooking until mixture reaches hard-ball stage (250°); remove from heat. In the bowl of a stand mixer, beat egg whites to stiff peaks. With mixer on high speed, pour sugar mixture in a thin stream over egg whites. Add vanilla and continue beating mixture 10 minutes or until it loses gloss and forms soft peaks. Stir in pecans and drop by rounded teaspoon onto wax paper, swirling each candy to a peak. Let sit overnight before eating.

Family Favorite

Southern Pecan Pie

3 eggs
⅔ cup sugar
Dash salt
1 cup dark corn syrup
⅓ cup melted butter (or margarine)
1 cup halved pecans
1 (9-inch) pie crust, unbaked

Preheat oven to 350°. In a mixing bowl, combine eggs, sugar, salt, corn syrup and butter, beating with an electric hand mixer until smooth. Stir in pecans and pour filling into pie crust. Bake 50 minutes or until a knife inserted into the filling comes out clean. Cool before serving.

Family Favorite

RESTAURANT INDEX

A

Ajax Diner 64
   Tamale Pie 65
   Turnip Green Dip 65
Aladdin Mediterranean Grill 142
Anchuca 184
   Anchuca Bonzo Recipe 184
Annie's Home Cooking 58
Aunt Jenny's Catfish Restaurant 220

B

Backwoods Bayou 130
   Bay & Bayou 130
   Coke Cola Cake 131
Bar-B-Q by Jim 70
   Baked Beans 71
Basil's 144
Batesville
   Dixieland BBQ 44
Bay Saint Louis
   Starfish Café 192
Bazar's Bakery & Breakfast 56
   Keto Chicken Lime Soup 57
   Spicy Avocado Toast 57
Beacon Restaurant, The 66
   Lemon Meringue Pie 67
Berry's Seafood & Catfish House 132
Big Fella's 36
   Crabmeat Cream Sauce 37
   Loaded Bake Beans 37
   Mustard Fried Fish 37

Biloxi
   Gollott's Fresh Catch Seafood 194
   Mary Mahoney's Old French House 196
   Petra Café 198
   Slap Ya Momma's 200
   Snapper's Seafood 202
   Taranto's Crawfish 204
   Tasty Tails Seafood House 206
   White Pillars Restaurant & Lounge 208
Black Dog Coffee & Café 180
Blue Biscuit, The 26
Booneville
   Market 105 46
Boo's Smokehouse Bar-B-Que 124
   Buttermilk Pie 125
Bouré Restaurant 68
   Bouré Sauce 69
   Grilled Peach Chutney 69
   Mississippi Caviar 69
Brandon
   Boo's Smokehouse Bar-B-Que 124
   Fresh Market Café 126
   Kismet's Restaurant 128
Brent's Drugs 146
   Brent's Chicken Salad 147
   Brent's Dreamsicle Shake 147
Brookhaven
   Backwoods Bayou 130

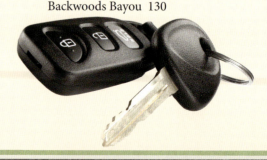

C

Café 7 38
Café Unique Home Cooking 86
   Butter Rolls 87
   Corn Salad 87
Camp Restaurant, The 168
   Bloody Mary 169
   Brisket Rub 168
   Sweet Heat BBQ Sauce 169
Carthage
   Singleton Steak & Fish House 84
Chatham
   Roy's Store 12
Checker Board, The 106
Christaphene's Bakery & Deli 40
   Cake Mix Cookies 41
   Four Layer Dessert 41
   Hot Cocoa 41
Clarksdale
   Hooker Grocer + Eatery 14
   Stone Pony Pizza 16
Cleveland
   J & W Smokehouse 18
   Scott's Hot Tamales 22
   Warehouse, The 20
Coffee Pot Café 92
   Crab Cakes 93
   Shrimp & Grits 93
Coffee Shop at Southern Turnings, The 236
   Crème Brulee Latte 237
   Glass Slipper, The 237
   Kat's Company Chicken 237
Columbus
   Café Unique Home Cooking 86
   Farmstead Restaurant 88
   Zachary's 90
Como
   Como Steakhouse, The 48
Como Steakhouse, The 48
   Como Delight 49
   Sausage & Cheese Plate 49
Connie's Fried Chicken 72
Corinth
   Pizza Grocery 50
Cotton Alley Café 170
   Chicken and Tasso 171
   Pasta Salad 171
Council House Restaurant 100
   Cream Cabbage Soup 101
   French Camp Bread 101
CrawBilly's on the Tracks 174
Crossroads Rib Shack 74
Crown Restaurant, The 28
   Chicken Allison 29
   Crown's Fresh Broccoli Salad, The 29
   Magnolia Macaroon Pie 28
Crystal Grill, The 24
   Pink Velvet Salad 25

D

Dat Kitchen Too 232
   BBQ Shrimp 233
   Meatloaf 232
Dinner Bell Café, The 234
   Citrus Cooler 235
   Doritos Casserole 235
   Sweet Potato Casserole 234
Dixieland BBQ 44

E

Eason's Fish House 164
   Loaded Jalapeños 165
   Pulled Pork Baked Potato 165
Enterprise
   Coffee Pot Café 92
Eslava's Grille 136
   Eslava's Sautee Zucchini and Squash 137
   Salmon in Lemon Caper Sauce 137
   Shrimp Scampi 137
Eupora
   Mama Guinn's Café 94

F

Farmstead Restaurant 88
  Lemon Parade 89
  Sweet Potato Casserole 89
Florence
  Berry's Seafood & Catfish House 132
  Jerry's Catfish House 134
Flowood
  Eslava's Grille 136
  Jo's Diner 138
  Soul Sistas' Diner 140
Food Hut, The 96
  Homemade Chicken Spaghetti 97
  Homemade Spaghetti 97
Forest
  Food Hut, The 96
  Fye Grubz 98
Foxworth
  Kane's Catfish, Seafood & Steakhouse 210
French Camp
  Council House Restaurant 100
Fresh Market Café 126
Frosty Mug 238
  Sea Foam 239
  Southern Pecan Pie 239
Fulmer's General Store 228
  Eggplant Casserole 229
  Vidalia Onion Casserole 229
Fulton
  Theo's Feed Mill 52
Fye Grubz 98
  Chicken Bacon Ranch Baked Potato 99
  Philly Cheese Sandwich 99

G

Gollott's Fresh Catch Seafood 194
  Seafood Gumbo 195
Greenville
  Scott's Hot Tamales 22
Greenwood
  Crystal Grill, The 24
Grenada
  333 Restaurant 54

Gulfport
  Murky Waters 212
Gumbo Girl 178
  Cajun Red Beans and Rice with Sausage 179
  Homemade Sweet Cornbread 179

H

Harvest Grill 108
  Grand Marnier Citrus Beignet 109
  Roasted Corn Salsa 109
Hattiesburg
  Movie Star Restaurant 214
  Murky Waters 212
  Petra Café 198
Hernando
  Bazar's Bakery & Breakfast 56
Hog Heaven Bar-B-Q 216
Holly Springs
  Annie's Home Cooking 58
  Marshall Steakhouse 60
  Phillips Grocery 62
Hollywood Café, The 34
  Buttermilk Pie 35
  Slow-Cooker Mississippi Pot Roast 35
Hooker Grocer + Eatery 14
  Hooker Collard Greens 15
  Parmesan, Cheddar & Green Onion Biscuits 15

I

Indianola
  Blue Biscuit, The 26
  Crown Restaurant, The 28
  Nola Restaurant 30
Iron Horse Grill 148

J

Jackson
   Aladdin Mediterranean Grill 142
   Basil's 144
   Brent's Drugs 146
   Iron Horse Grill 148
   Keifer's Downtown 150
   Martin's Downtown 152
   Old Capitol Inn 154
   Pig & Pint, The 156
   Rooster's Restaurant 158
Jerry's Catfish House 134
Jo's Diner 138
J & W Smokehouse 18
   Pecan Pie 19
   Spaghetti 19

K

Kane's Catfish, Seafood & Steakhouse 210
Keifer's Downtown 150
   Hummus 151
   White Chili 151
Kismet's Restaurant 128

L

Laurel
   Hog Heaven Bar-B-Q 216
   Pearl's Diner 218
Leatha's Bar-B-Que Inn 226
   Smoked Salmon Fillets 227
   Smoked Turkey Legs 227
Lee's Steakhouse 114
   Campers Dish 114
   Grilled Whole Petite Green Beans 115
   Mac & Cheese 115
Little Dooey, The 116
   Gannie's Jalapeño Grits 117
   Turnip Green Casserole Surprise 117
Louisville
   Market Café 102

M

Madison
   Mama Hamil's Southern Cooking & BBQ, Inc. 160
   Strawberry Café, The 162
Magee
   Berry's Seafood & Catfish House 132
Mama Guinn's Café 94
   Fried Dill Pickles 95
   Fruit Top Biscuits 95
Mama Hamil's Southern Cooking & BBQ, Inc. 160
   Large Pound Cake 161
   Williamsburg Orange Cake 161
Mantee
   Pop's Family Diner 104
Market 105 46
   Bread Pudding with Irish Cream Sauce 47
   Chicken & Dumplings 47
Market Café 102
   Crab Cakes 103
   Mexican Street Tacos 103
Marshall Steakhouse 60
   Kahlua Cake 61
   Maryland Crabcakes 61
   Smoked Salmon Dip 60
Martin's Downtown 152
   Lemon Butter Broccoli Parmesan 153
   Three Cheese Pimento Cheese 153
Mary Mahoney's Old French House 196
   Bread Pudding 197
Mendenhall
   Eason's Fish House 164
   Smokey Mountain Grille & Rib Shack 166
Meridian
   Checker Board, The 106
   Harvest Grill 108
   Weidmann's Restaurant 110
Merigold
   Crawdad's Restaurant 32
Moss Creek Fish House 172
Movie Star Restaurant 214
   Green Bean Almondine 215
   Killer Chicken 215
Murky Waters 212

N

Natchez
   Camp Restaurant, The 168
   Cotton Alley Café 170
Neon Pig 76
   Pimento Cheese 77
   Potato Salad 77
Newton
   T-Bones, Too 112
Nola Restaurant 30
   Crawfish Dirty Rice 31
   Grits and Grillades 31

O

Ocean Springs
   Aunt Jenny's Catfish Restaurant 220
   Murky Waters 212
   Shed Barbeque & Blues Joint, The 222
   Vestige 224
Old Capitol Inn 154
Oxford
   Ajax Diner 64
   Beacon Restaurant, The 66
   Bouré Restaurant 68

P

Pearl
   Fresh Market Café 126
   Moss Creek Fish House 172
Pearl's Diner 218
   Ms Pearl's Chicken Spaghetti 219
   Ms Pearl's Pot Roast with Potatoes & Carrots 219
Pelahatchie
   CrawBilly's on the Tracks 174
Petal
   Leatha's Bar-B-Que Inn 226
Petra Café 198
   Cauliflower with Tahini Sauce 199
   Chicken Shawarma 199
Phillips Grocery 62
Pig & Pint, The 156
Pizza Grocery 50
   Meatballs 51
   Pimento Cheese Fritters 51

Pop's Family Diner 104
   House-Made Ranch 105
   Shrimp Boil Hobo Pack 105

R

Richland
   Tom's Fried Pies 176
Richton
   Fulmer's General Store 228
Ridgeland
   Gumbo Girl 178
Robinsonville
   Hollywood Café, The 34
Rolling Fork
   Big Fella's 36
Romie's Grocery 78
Rooster's Restaurant 158
   Creole Tomato Gravy 159
Roy's Store 12

S

Scott's Hot Tamales 22
   Hot Tamale and Cabbage Casserole 23
   Salisbury Steak 22
   Tamale Delight 23
Sebastopol
   Lee's Steakhouse 114
Seminary
   Shady Acres Village 230
Shady Acres Village 230
   Cheesy Potato Soup 231
   Cream Cheese Chili 231
   Hash Brown Casserole 231
Shed Barbeque & Blues Joint, The 222
   Brad's Award-Winning Slow-Smoked Brisket 223
   Southern Dry Rub 223
Singleton Steak & Fish House 84
   Coconut Custard Pie 85
   Old-Time Buttermilk Pie 85
Slap Ya Momma's 200
   Pork Belly Burnt Ends 201
   Smoked Jalapeño Poppers 201
   Ultimate Nachos 201
Smokey Mountain Grille & Rib Shack 166
   Baked Bean Base 167
   Jalapeño Jelly 167, 179

Smoked Chicken Salad 167
Snapper's Seafood 202
Soul Sistas' Diner 140
Starfish Café 192
Starkville
   Little Dooey, The 116
Stone Pony Pizza 16
Strawberry Café, The 162
   Crab Chowder (Bisque) 163
   Sweet Potato Smash 163
Sweet Tea & Biscuits 80
   Homemade Biscuits 81
   Strawberry Pretzel Salad 81

T

Taranto's Crawfish 204
   Bread Pudding 205
   Coleslaw 205
Tasty Tails Seafood House 206
   Boiled Crawfish 207
   Red Beans & Rice 207
T-Bones Steakhouse 118
T-Bones, Too 112
   Chicken Taco Casserole 113
Ten 10 South Rooftop Bar & Gril 182
   10 South Comeback Sauce 183
   10 South Crab Cakes 183
Theo's Feed Mill 52
Three 333 Restaurant 54
   333 1000 Island Dressing 55
   333 House-Made Ranch Salad Dressing 55
Tomato Place, The 186
   Chocolate Bread Pudding 187
   Tomato Place Pie 187
Tom's Fried Pies 176
   Breakfast Casserole 177
   Kayla's Homemade Ice Cream 177
   Mallory's Banana Pudding 177
Tupelo
   Bar-B-Q by Jim 70
   Connie's Fried Chicken 72
   Crossroads Rib Shack 74
   Neon Pig 76
   Romie's Grocery 78
   Sweet Tea & Biscuits 80
Tylertown
   Black Dog Coffee & Café 180

U

Union
   T-Bones Steakhouse 118
Urban Country Kitchen 120
   Caramel Cake 121
   Urban Country's Fried Chicken 120

V

Vestige 224
Vicksburg
   10 South Rooftop Bar & Gril 182
   Anchuca 184
   Tomato Place, The 186
   Walnut Hills 188

W

Walnut Grove
   Urban Country Kitchen 120
Walnut Hills 188
   Walnut Hills Bourbon Pie 189
Warehouse, The 20
Waveland
   Dat Kitchen Too 232
Waynesboro
   Dinner Bell Café, The 234
Weidmann's Restaurant 110
White Pillars Restaurant & Lounge 208
   Oyster Hand Pies 209
   Smokehouse Gumbo 209
Wiggins
   Coffe Shop at Southern Turnings, The 236
   Frosty Mug 238

Y

Yazoo City
   Café 7 38
   Christaphene's Bakery & Deli 40

Z

Zachary's 90
   Loaded Potato Soup 91
   Roasted Red Pepper Hummus 91

RECIPE INDEX

A

Anchuca Bonzo Recipe 184
Appetizers
  Crab Dip 111
  Deviled Eggs 217
  Fried Dill Pickles 95
  Mississippi Caviar 69
  Pimento Cheese 77
  Roasted Red Pepper Hummus 91
  Smoked Salmon Dip 60
  Tomato Dip 17
  Turnip Green Dip 65
  Ultimate Nachos 201
Apples
  Apple-Raisin Slaw 141
  Brandied Fruit 79
  Caramel Apple Pecan Squares 149
  Fried Apple Rings 107
Avacados
  Keto Chicken Lime Soup 57
  Mississippi Caviar 69
  Spicy Avocado Toast 57

B

Bacony Baked Beans 175
Baked Bean Base 167
Baked French Toast Casserole 127
Banana
  Banana Mallow Pie 63
  Banana Nut Bread 13
  Mallory's Banana Pudding 177
Barbecue Cups 21
Barbecued Spareribs 175
Barbecue Sauce 73
Bay & Bayou 130
BBQ Shrimp 233
Beans
  Bacony Baked Beans 175
  Baked Beans 71
  Cajun Red Beans and Rice with Sausage 179
  Grilled Whole Petite Green Beans 115
  Hummus 151
  Loaded Baked Beans 37
  Mississippi Caviar 69
  Red Beans & Rice 207
  Ultimate Nachos 201
Beef. *See also* Sausage
  Beef Biscuit Roll 193
  Brad's Award-Winning Slow-Smoked Brisket 223
  Burger Pockets 73
  Campers Dish 114
  Corned Beef Hash Frittata 27
  Creamed Chip Beef 75
  Doritos Casserole 235
  Enchilada Casserole 211
  Ground Sirloin Dinner 129
  Impossible Taco Pie 141
  Liver and Onions 225

Meatballs 51
Meatloaf 181, 232
Mexican Street Tacos 103
Ms. Pearl's Pot Roast with Potatoes & Carrots 219
Old School Burgers 33
Oyster Hand Pies 209
Philly Cheese Sandwich 99
Reuben Casserole 213
Salisbury Steak 22
Slow-Cooker Mississippi Pot Roast 35
Spaghetti 19
Best-Ever Pecan Pie 225
Beverage
  Bloody Mary 169
  Brent's Dreamsicle Shake 147
  Citrus Cooler 235
  Crème Brûlée Latte 237
  Holiday Punch 45
  Hot Cocoa 41
  The Glass Slipper 237
Biscuit
  Barbecue Cups 21
  Beef Biscuit Roll 193
  Breakfast Biscuits 13
  Burger Pockets 73
  Fruit Top Biscuits 95
  Homemade Biscuits 81
Blender Custard Pie 155
Bloody Mary 169
Blueberry Cake 139
Boiled Crawfish 207
Bourbon Balls 211
Bouré Sauce 69
Brad's Award-Winning Slow-Smoked Brisket 223
Braised Mushrooms 221
Brandied Fruit 79
Bread. *See also* Biscuit, Cornbread
  10 South Crab Cakes 183
  Banana Nut Bread 13
  Barbecue Cups 21
  Bread Pudding 197, 205
  Bread Pudding with Irish Cream Sauce 47
  Breakfast Casserole 177
  Butter Rolls 87
  Cheese Bread 63
  Chocolate Bread Pudding 187
  Crab Cakes 93
  Dutch Baby 53

French Camp Bread 101
Grand Marnier Citrus Beignet 109
Hot Breakfast Rolls 139
Maryland Crabcakes 61
Mashed Potato Casserole 173
Meatballs 51
Meatloaf 232
Old School Burgers 33
Oyster Hand Pies 209
Parmesan, Cheddar and Green Onion Biscuits 15
Pimento Cheese Fritters 51
Reuben Casserole 213
Salisbury Steak 22
Tomato Place Pie 187
Breakfast
  Breakfast Biscuits 13
  Breakfast Casserole 177
  Dutch Baby 53
  Hot Breakfast Rolls 139
  Spicy Avocado Toast 57
Brent's Chicken Salad 147
Brent's Dreamsicle Shake 147
Brisket Rub 168
Burger Pockets 73
Burgers, Old School 33
Butter Fingers 39
Buttermilk Pie 35, 125
Buttermilk Pie, Old-Time 85

C

Cabbage
  Coleslaw 205
  Cream Cabbage Soup 101
  Deconstructed Cabbage Rolls 21
  Greek Coleslaw 173
  Hot Tamale and Cabbage Casserole 23
Cajun Red Beans and Rice with Sausage 179
Cake
  Anchuca Bonzo Recipe 184
  Blueberry Cake 139
  Caramel Cake 121
  Coke Cola Cake 131
  Kahlua Cake 61
  Large Pound Cake 161
  Twinkie Cake 17
  Williamsburg Orange Cake 161
Campers Dish 114
Caramel Apple Pecan Squares 149
Caramel Cake 121
Carrots
  Creole Tomato Gravy 159
  Ham Hash 203
  Hooker Collard Greens 15
  Killer Chicken 215
  Ms. Pearl's Pot Roast with Potatoes & Carrots 219
  Roasted Root Vegetables 53
Cauliflower with Tahini Sauce 199
Cheese Bread 63
Cheese Marbles 79
Cheesy Potato Soup 231
Chicken
  Brent's Chicken Salad 147
  Chicken Allison 29
  Chicken and Tasso 171
  Chicken-Bacon-Ranch Baked Potato 99
  Chicken Bog 75
  Chicken & Dumplings 47
  Chicken Shawarma 199
  Chicken Taco Casserole 113
  Homemade Chicken Spaghetti 97
  Kat's Company Chicken 237
  Keto Chicken Lime Soup 57
  Killer Chicken 215
  Ms. Pearl's Chicken Spaghetti 219
  No-Peek Chicken 129
  Smoked Chicken Salad 167
  Smokehouse Gumbo 209
  Urban Country's Fried Chicken 120
  White Chili 151
Chili
  Cream Cheese Chili 231
  Homemade Chili 203
  White Chili 151
Chocolate
  Anchuca Bonzo Recipe 184
  Bourbon Balls 211
  Bread Pudding 205
  Chocolate Bread Pudding 187
  Como Delight 49
  Easy Chocolate Pie 193
  Four-Layer Dessert 41
  Hot Cocoa 41
  Kahlua Cake 61
  The Glass Slipper 237
  Walnut Hills Bourbon Pie 189
Citrus Cooler 235
Coconut Custard Pie 85
Coke Cola Cake 131
Coleslaw 205
Coleslaw, Greek 173
Como Delight 49
Corn
  Corn Salad 87
  Cream Cheese Chili 231
  Mississippi Baked Corn 27
  Roasted Corn Salsa 109
  Skillet-Style Mexican Street Corn 133
  Tamale Pie 65
Cornbread
  Cornbread Salad 59
  Homemade Sweet Cornbread 179
  Southern Cornbread 157
Corned Beef Hash Frittata 27
Crab
  10 South Crab Cakes 183
  Crab Cakes 93, 103
  Crab Chowder (Bisque) 163
  Crab Dip 111
  Crabmeat Cream Sauce 37
  Deviled Crab 33
  Maryland Crabcakes 61
  Seafood Gumbo 195

Crawfish
  Boiled Crawfish 207
  Crawfish Dirty Rice 31
  Maryland Crabcakes 61
Cream Cabbage Soup 101
Creamed Chip Beef 75
Creamed Onions 143
Crème Brûlée Latte 237
Creole Tomato Gravy 159
Crown's Fresh Broccoli Salad, The 29

D

Dessert. *See also* Cakes, Pies, Puddings
  Anchuca Bonzo Recipe 184
  Brandied Fruit 79
  Butter Fingers 39
  Cake Mix Cookies 41
  Como Delight 49
  Four-Layer Dessert 41
  Kayla's Homemade Ice Cream 177
  Lemon Parade 89
  Peanut Butter Fudge 155
  Sea Foam 239
  Snowballs 149
  Twinkie Cake 17
Deviled Crab 33
Deviled Eggs 217
Dill Pickles, Fried 95
Doritos Casserole 235
Dressing
  333 1000 Island Dressing 55
  333 House-Made Ranch Salad Dressing 55
  House-Made Ranch 105
Dutch Baby 53

E

Easy Chocolate Pie 193
Eggplant Casserole 229
Enchilada Casserole 211
Eslava's Sautée Zucchini and Squash 137

F

Fish
  Baked Fish 143
  Bay & Bayou 130
  Mustard Fried Fish 37
  Salmon in Lemon Caper Sauce 137
  Smoked Salmon Dip 60
  Smoked Salmon Fillets 227
Four-Layer Dessert 41
French Camp Bread 101

G

Gannie's Jalapeño Grits 117
Glass Slipper, The 237
Grand Marnier Citrus Beignet 109
Green Bean Almondine 215
Grilled Peach Chutney 69
Grilled Whole Petite Green Beans 115
Grits
  Gannie's Jalapeño Grits 117
  Grits and Grillades 31
  Shrimp & Grits 93
Ground Sirloin Dinner 129

H

Ham
  Ham, Cheese & Rice 107
  Ham Dogs 127
  Ham Hash 203
Hash Brown Casserole 231
Herbed Rice 217
Holiday Punch 45
Homemade Chili 203
Homemade Sweet Cornbread 179
Hooker Collard Greens 15
Hot Cocoa 41
House-Made Ranch 105
Hummus 151

I

Impossible Taco Pie 141

J

Jalapeño
   Bacony Baked Beans 175
   Cajun Red Beans and Rice with Sausage 179
   Gannie's Jalapeño Grits 117
   Jalapeño Jelly 167
   Keto Chicken Lime Soup 57
   Loaded Jalapeños 165
   Smoked Jalapeño Poppers 201
   Tamale Delight 23

K

Kahlua Cake 61
Kale, Pan-Fried 145
Kat's Company Chicken 237
Kayla's Homemade Ice Cream 177
Keto Chicken Lime Soup 57
Killer Chicken 215
Kum Back Sauce 213

L

Large Pound Cake 161
Lemon Butter Broccoli Parmesan 153
Lemon Meringue Pie 67
Lemon Parade 89
Liver and Onions 225
Loaded Baked Beans 37
Loaded Jalapeños 165
Loaded Potato Soup 91

M

Mac & Cheese 115
Magnolia Macaroon Pie 28
Mallory's Banana Pudding 177
Maple-Bacon Brussels Sprouts 111
Maryland Crabcakes 61
Mashed Potato Casserole 173
Meatballs 51
Meatloaf 181, 232
Mexican Street Tacos 103
Mississippi Caviar 69
Ms. Pearl's Chicken Spaghetti 219
Ms. Pearl's Pot Roast with Potatoes & Carrots 219
Mustard Fried Fish 37

N

No-Peek Chicken 129
Nuts. *See also* Pecan
   Banana Nut Bread 13
   Butter Fingers 39
   Green Bean Almondine 215
   Williamsburg Orange Cake 161

O

Oyster Stew 145

P

Parmesan, Cheddar and Green Onion Biscuits 15
Pasta
   Campers Dish 114
   Homemade Chicken Spaghetti 97
   Homemade Spaghetti 97
   Mac & Cheese 115
   Ms. Pearl's Chicken Spaghetti 219
   Pasta Salad 171
   Shrimp Delight 39
   Spaghetti 19
Peanut Butter Fudge 155
Pecan
   Best-Ever Pecan Pie 225
   Bourbon Balls 211
   Bread Pudding 205
   Como Delight 49

Four-Layer Dessert 41
  Lemon Parade 89
  Pecan Pie 19
  Pink Velvet Salad 25
  Southern Pecan Pie 239
  Sweet Potato Casserole 234
Philly Cheese Sandwich 99
Pie
  Banana Mallow Pie 63
  Best-Ever Pecan Pie 225
  Blender Custard Pie 155
  Buttermilk Pie 35, 125
  Easy Chocolate Pie 193
  Impossible Taco Pie 141
  Lemon Meringue Pie 67
  Lemon Parade 89
  Magnolia Macaroon Pie 28
  Old-Time Buttermilk Pie 85
  Oyster Hand Pies 209
  Pecan Pie 19
  Southern Pecan Pie 239
  Tamale Pie 65
  Tomato Place Pie 187
  Walnut Hills Bourbon Pie 189
Pimento Cheese 77
Pimento Cheese Fritters 51
Pineapple
  Brandied Fruit 79
  Pink Velvet Salad 25
  Twinkie Cake 17
Pink Velvet Salad 25
Pork. See also Ham, Sausage
  Bacony Baked Beans 175
  Baked Bean Base 167
  Baked Beans 71
  Barbecued Spareribs 175
  Chicken and Tasso 171
  Chicken-Bacon-Ranch Baked Potato 99
  Cornbread Salad 59
  Cream Cabbage Soup 101
  Grilled Peach Chutney 69
  Hooker Collard Greens 15
  Kat's Company Chicken 237
  Liver and Onions 225
  Loaded Jalapeños 165
  Maple-Bacon Brussels Sprouts 111
  Pork Belly Burnt Ends 201
  Pulled Pork Baked Potato 165

  Red Beans & Rice 207
  Red Rice 221
  Smoked Jalapeño Poppers 201
  Tamale Pie 65
  Tomato Place Pie 187
  Ultimate Nachos 201
Potato
  Cheesy Potato Soup 231
  Chicken-Bacon-Ranch Baked Potato 99
  Corned Beef Hash Frittata 27
  Golden Brown Potatoes 157
  Ground Sirloin Dinner 129
  Ham Hash 203
  Hash Brown Casserole 231
  Killer Chicken 215
  Loaded Potato Soup 91
  Luscious Potato Casserole 181
  Mashed Potato Casserole 173
  Ms. Pearl's Pot Roast with Potatoes & Carrots 219
  Potato Pancakes 133
  Potato Salad 77
  Pulled Pork Baked Potato 165
  Roasted Root Vegetables 53
  Shrimp Boil Hobo Packs 105
  Spicy Grilled Potatoes 119
  Sweet Potato Casserole 89, 234
  Sweet Potato Smash 163
Pot Roast, Slow-Cooker Mississippi 35
Pudding
  Bread Pudding 197, 205
  Bread Pudding with Irish Cream Sauce 47
  Chocolate Bread Pudding 187
  Como Delight 49
  Mallory's Banana Pudding 177
  Rice Pudding 119
  Pulled Pork Baked Potato 165

R

Red Beans & Rice 207
Red Rice 221
Reuben Casserole 213
Rice
  Bay & Bayou 130
  Cajun Red Beans and Rice with Sausage 179
  Crawfish Dirty Rice 31
  Ham, Cheese & Rice 107
  Herbed Rice 217
  No-Peek Chicken 129
  Red Beans & Rice 207
  Red Rice 221
  Rice Pudding 119
  Seafood Gumbo 195
  Smokehouse Gumbo 209
  Vidalia Onion Casserole 229
Roasted Corn Salsa 109
Roasted Red Pepper Hummus 91
Roasted Root Vegetables 53
Rolls, Butter 87
Rolls, Hot Breakfast 139

S

Salads
  Brent's Chicken Salad 147
  Cornbread Salad 59
  Corn Salad 87
  Mississippi Caviar 69
  Pasta Salad 171
  Pink Velvet Salad 25
  Potato Salad 77
  Smoked Chicken Salad 167
  Strawberry Pretzel Salad 81
  The Crown's Fresh Broccoli Salad 29
Salisbury Steak 22
Sauce
  10 South Comeback Sauce 183
  Baked Bean Base 167
  Barbecue Sauce 73
  Bouré Sauce 69
  Cauliflower with Tahini Sauce 199
  Crabmeat Cream Sauce 37
  Irish Cream Sauce 47
  Kum Back Sauce 213
  Rum Sauce Topping 197
  Sweet Heat BBQ Sauce 169
Sausage
  Baked Beans 71
  Cajun Red Beans and Rice with Sausage 179
  Crawfish Dirty Rice 31
  Grilled Whole Petite Green Beans 115
  Hooker Collard Greens 15
  Loaded Baked Beans 37
  Red Beans & Rice 207
  Sausage & Cheese Plate 49
  Shrimp Boil Hobo Packs 105
  Smokehouse Gumbo 209
Sea Foam 239
Seafood. *See also* Crab, Crawfish, Fish, Shrimp
  Oyster Stew 145
  Seafood Gumbo 195

Shrimp
  BBQ Shrimp 233
  Seafood Gumbo 195
  Shrimp Boil Hobo Packs 105
  Shrimp Delight 39
  Shrimp & Grits 93
  Shrimp Pie 45
  Shrimp Scampi 137
Skillet-Style Mexican Street Corn 133
Smoked Chicken Salad 167
Smoked Jalapeño Poppers 201
Smoked Salmon Dip 60
Smoked Salmon Fillets 227
Smokehouse Gumbo 209
Snowballs 149
Soup
  Cheesy Potato Soup 231
  Keto Chicken Lime Soup 57
  Loaded Potato Soup 91
Southern Dry Rub 223
Southern Pecan Pie 239
Spaghetti 19
Spaghetti, Homemade 97
Spicy Avocado Toast 57
Spicy Grilled Potatoes 119
Strawberry Pretzel Salad 81
Sweet Potato Casserole 89, 234
Sweet Potato Smash 163

T

10 South Comeback Sauce 183
10 South Crab Cakes 183
333 1000 Island Dressing 55
333 House-Made Ranch Salad Dressing 55
Three Cheese Pimento Cheese 153
Tomato Dip 17
Tomato Place Pie 187
Turkey Legs, Smoked 227
Turnip Green Casserole Surprise 117
Turnip Green Dip 65
Twinkie Cake 17

U

Ultimate Nachos 201
Urban Country's Fried Chicken 120

V

Vidalia Onion Casserole 229

W

Walnut Hills Bourbon Pie 189
White Chili 151

Want More Recipes?

Bonus Recipes

Add Your Own

My Kitchen Wall

Great American Cookbooks
Everyday Recipes for the Everyday Cook

My Notebook Series
$14.95 • wire-o-bound • 5⅜ x 8¼ • 192 pages

Alabama • Georgia • Mississippi

Farm to Table Fabulous
$18.95 • 256 pages • 7x9
paperbound • full color

Busy Moms: A Farm to Table Fabulous Cookbook
$18.95 • 256 pages • 7x9
paperbound • full color

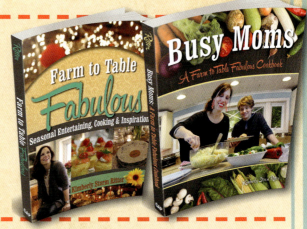

State BACK ROAD RESTAURANT Recipes

From two-lane highways and interstates to dirt roads and quaint downtowns, here's well-researched and charming guides to each state's best back road restaurants.

EACH: *$21.95 • 256 pages • 7x9 • paperbound • full color*

**Alabama • Kentucky • Louisiana • Mississippi
Missouri • North Carolina • Oklahoma
South Carolina • Tennessee • Texas**

Church Recipes are the Best

Georgia Church Suppers

$18.95 • 256 pages
7x10 paperbound • full color

Mississippi Church Suppers

$21.95 • 288 pages
7x10 paperbound • full color

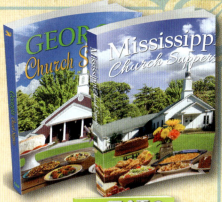

Eat & Explore State Cookbook Series

Discover community celebrations and unique destinations, as they share their favorite recipes.

EACH: *$18.95 • 256 pages*
7x9 • paperbound • full color

**Arkansas • Illinois • North Carolina
Ohio • Oklahoma • Virginia**

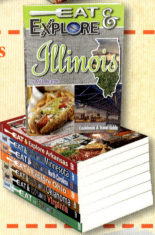

Kids in the Kitchen

$18.95 • 256 pages
7x10 • paperbound • full color

Little Gulf Coast Seafood Cookbook

$14.95 • 192 pages
5½x8½ paperbound • full color

State Hometown Cookbook Series

A Hometown Taste of America, One State at a Time

EACH: *$21.95 • 240 to 272 pages*
7x10 • paperbound • full color

**Alabama • Georgia • Louisiana • Mississippi
South Carolina • Tennessee • Texas • West Virginia**

Blog

Cookbooks

Recipes

Visit us online for:

Bonus Recipes • Cooking Tips • Great American News • Exclusive Discounts

www.GreatAmericanPublishers.com

Join the **We Love 2 Cook Club** and get a 10% discount.